新编实用商务英语口语教程

主编 石莉莉

苏州大学出版社
Soochow University Press

图书在版编目(CIP)数据

新编实用商务英语口语教程 = New Practical Oral English for Business / 石莉莉主编. —— 苏州：苏州大学出版社，2018.8（2021.12 重印）
ISBN 978-7-5672-2403-2

Ⅰ.①新… Ⅱ.①石… Ⅲ.①商务—英语—口语—教材 Ⅳ.①F7

中国版本图书馆 CIP 数据核字(2018)第 073679 号

书　　名：	新编实用商务英语口语教程
主　　编：	石莉莉
责任编辑：	王　娅
策划编辑：	王　娅
装帧设计：	刘　俊
出版发行：	苏州大学出版社（Soochow University Press）
社　　址：	苏州市十梓街 1 号　邮编：215006
印　　装：	广东虎彩云印刷有限公司
网　　址：	www.sudapress.com
E - mail：	305303279@qq.com
邮购热线：	0512-67480030
销售热线：	0512-67481020
开　　本：	700mm×1000mm　印张：9.25　字数：166 千
版　　次：	2018 年 8 月第 1 版
印　　次：	2021 年 12 月第 3 次印刷
书　　号：	ISBN 978-7-5672-2403-2
定　　价：	32.00 元

凡购本社图书发现印装错误，请与本社联系调换。服务热线：0512-67481020

《新编实用商务英语口语教程》
编委会

- 主　编　石莉莉
- 副主编　张小琴　倪　玥
- 顾　问　李　萍
- 审　核　李更春
- 成　员　杨　银　徐爱华　吕　雯
  　　　　杨　翔　王万荣　石　瑶
  　　　　陈　晨

前言

随着当今经济全球化及我国"一带一路"倡议的推进,社会对能够熟练掌握商务英语知识与技能,从事国际商务活动的人才的需求日益增加。近几年来,商务英语专业发展迅速,《高等学校商务英语专业本科教学要求(试行)》对商务英语专业的人才培养目标、专业知识与能力构成、课程设置做了明确的要求,用以指导商务英语专业建设及课程建设。

商务英语口语是商务英语专业学生应具备的语言技能之一,其作为一种专门用途英语,有特殊的表达方式和使用场合,具有较强的专业性和应用性。《新编实用商务英语口语教程》一书将商务实践与英语语言技能有机结合,以"服务交际"为原则,内容涵盖商务工作所涉及的日常交际、涉外活动和涉外业务等常见场景,以功能用途划分,通过商务模拟情境,让学生进行商务口语训练。

本教材共有12个单元,围绕国际贸易的主要商务活动,选取商务接待、礼仪祝词、商务旅行、商务谈判、商务访问、商务陈述、企业介绍、市场营销、商务会议、国际会展等主题编写。每个单元围绕中心主题设计情境对话和实践活动,从词、句、情景对话、话题讨论到自主对话以及拓展阅读,由简入繁,循序渐进,体现了英语与商务的融合性及应用性。单元中通过任务设置,明确模拟实践内容,提高学生商务英语语言的实践应用能力和解决问题的能力。

教材遵循以学生为中心和任务型教学的理念,可以满足本科院校商务英语、国际贸易、国际商务和"3+4"中职—本科商务英语等相关专业的学生,从事国际商务工作的外经贸从业人员、外事人员以及广大英语爱好者的需要。

本书编写组
2017年11月

Contents

Unit One   Protocol Routine   / 1
Unit Two   Dinner Party   / 12
Unit Three   Business Travel   / 21
Unit Four   Business Interview   / 33
Unit Five   Business Presentation   / 44
Unit Six   Enterprise Introduction   / 57
Unit Seven   Marketing & Promotion   / 71
Unit Eight   Business Negotiation   / 83
Unit Nine   Business Meeting   / 93
Unit Ten   International Exhibition   / 104
Unit Eleven   Public Relations   / 117
Unit Twelve   Transportation & Logistics   / 126
Keys   / 135

Unit One   Protocol Routine

Unit One

Protocol Routine

 Unit objectives

After learning this unit, you should
- be able to find ways to improve your oral skills and performance;
- master the basic words and expressions about protocol routine;
- know some cultural background knowledge about protocol routine.

Preparing

I. **Useful words and expressions**

1. 接机
2. 久仰大名
3. 旅途愉快
4. 不远万里
5. 推荐
6. 为……设宴洗尘
7. 向……告别
8. 美好回忆
9. 很荣幸……
10. 保持联系
11. souvenir
12. the symbol of …
13. welcome speech
14. farewell speech
15. hospitality
16. thoughtful arrangement
17. check in
18. everything goes smoothly
19. claim baggage
20. adjust to the time difference

II. **Useful sentences**

1. I am here to meet you.
2. I have heard it for a long time.
3. Let me first help you check in.
4. It's a pity that you are leaving us.
5. I wish you a pleasant journey.

Situational conversations

Receiving the guest

A: Excuse me, are you Mr. Yu from America?

B: Oh, yes, I am.

A: How do you do, Mr. Yu. My name is Brian. I am the receptionist of ABC Company and I am here to meet you.

B: How do you do, and thank you very much for meeting me here.

A: You're welcome. And I will be your guide during your stay in Shanghai.

B: That's wonderful! Thanks a lot.
A: By the way, how was your journey?
B: Oh, everything went smoothly, so I don't feel tired at all.
A: Well, that's very good. Will you please take your baggage and follow me? The bus is waiting outside for us.
B: Sure. Let's hurry!

Way to the hotel

A: So, Mr. Yu, have you got a plan yet?
B: Oh, please call me Jacky. Actually, I haven't made it, but I think you can give me some good ideas.
A: Of course. I would like to recommend the Oriental Pearl TV Towel. It's one of the symbols of Shanghai.
B: Oh, yes. I have heard of it for a long time.
A: Besides the towel, the Bund and Yu Garden are also good choices for you. Please let me make a plan for you.
B: Oh, that's very kind of you, Brian.
A: My pleasure.
B: Oh. Here we are. Let me first help you check in. And then you can have a short rest in your room. After that I will meet you in the restaurant at 11:20.
A: Thank you for doing all this for me.
B: You're welcome.

Seeing off the guest

A: It's a pity that you are leaving us.
B: I feel sorry to leave you, too.
A: Have you checked in?
B: No, not yet.
A: Now, let's go through Customs. This way, please. Here is something I'd like you to keep as a souvenir.
B: Thank you. I'll open it. Oh! It is a Chinese painting. It's really marvelous.

The horses are so nice.

A: I am glad you like it. I hope it will remind you of me and our friendship.

B: I don't know how to thank you for your kindness.

A: I appreciate very much everything you've done for us. I wish I could repay you somehow.

B: It's my pleasure.

A: Listen! It's announcing the departure of your flight.

B: Right. I have to go now.

A: I wish you a pleasant journey.

B: Hope to see you again.

A: Goodbye. And don't forget to keep in touch.

Oral practice

I. Talk with each other about the following questions or topics

1. How to make a satisfactory tour schedule?
2. What kind of quality (qualities) should a tour guide have?
3. How to deal with the requirements of different tourists?
4. As a tour guide, what is the most important thing you should do when touring?

II. Situational practice

1. Mr. Carl Smith has an appointment with the general manager of TCL Company, Mr. Li, who is in a meeting at the moment. The receptionist of TCL Company, Xiaowang, greets the visitor and starts a conversation with him.

2. An assistant manager of Huawei Company, Mr. Huang, goes to the airport to welcome Peter O'Donnell, a trainee manager in the head office in New York. Mr. Huang greets Peter, introduces himself and makes a small talk with Peter. On the way to the hotel, Mr. Huang introduces the city and some places of interest to Peter O'Donnell.

Complementary reading

Text A

Etiquette

Etiquette covers a set of rules for a variety of interactions and situations. In all business dealings, you should practice proper etiquette to leave the right impression on those around you. Business etiquette can be a bit more formal than personal etiquette. Ignoring basic business etiquette might be detrimental to your business reputation and career. Especially in management and leadership positions, employees should strive to set a good example for other employees in the business.

Phone

Always identify the company and your name when you answer your business phone. A standard greeting such as "Hello, this is John Doe of XYZ Company" is an appropriate greeting. When you make calls to others, always identify yourself and your company. Speak clearly and avoid working on other tasks while you are on the phone. You should never eat, drink or hold outside conversations while you are speaking on the phone.

Email

Even though emails seem to be informal, business emails should maintain a sense of formality. Use greetings, proper punctuation, grammar and closings. Proofread all emails before you send them, and even read them aloud in some cases to check the tone of the message. Avoid using all capitals in an email, which is seen as yelling. Text abbreviations and emoticons have no place in business communications. Review the "to" field before sending to ensure you have chosen the right recipient.

Daily Interactions

Always speak to coworkers and others in the workplace when you arrive. Smile at people you pass in the hallway and exchange friendly greetings such as a quick "How are you?" as you pass by offices in the building. Avoid telling jokes that might come off as inappropriate and generally avoid the topics of politics and religion while at work. Make yourself approachable to your peers and promptly return phone calls and emails.

Meetings

When you attend meetings, arrive a few minutes earlier with a notepad and pen in hand. Do not talk on your phone, read text messages or emails, or otherwise distract yourself from what is happening. Always speak in turn and do not interrupt when other people are speaking. Take notes, but do not doodle or show boredom during the meeting. Keep your attention focused on the agenda and the speaker.

Business Meals

Attempt to find out beforehand who will be paying for a meal if you are unsure. If you are taking clients out to dinner, it is customary for the business to handle the check. Place your napkin on your lap, rise whenever ladies excuse themselves from the table if you are a man, and use "please" and "thank you" with the wait staff. Avoid ordering food that is messy or requires you to eat with your hands. Take small bites and cut only the amount of food you will eat in one bite. When you are finished, cross your silverware across your plate, but keep your napkin in your lap.

Text B

Your Honor Mr. Mayor, My Chinese Friends, Ladies and Gentlemen,

I feel honored to come here on my first visit to your beautiful city. On behalf of all the members of my mission, I would like to take this opportunity to express our sincere thanks to our host for their earnest invitation and gracious hospitality we have received since we set foot on this charming land. I am also very happy that this visit has given me an excellent opportunity to convey to you and to the people of Shanghai warm greetings and sincere good wishes of the government and people of my country. Although we live with a distance of thousands of miles between us, "long distance separates no bosom friends", as one of your Tang dynasty poets said.

Here, I would like to extend in person our official invitation to the mayor of Shanghai. We would like His Honor to visit our city at his earliest convenience, so as to give us an opportunity to return the warm reception and hospitality we enjoy here.

I greatly cherish the close relationship between our two cities. I also greatly value the position we enjoy as one of your most important trading partners. In spite of the worldwide economic recession in recent years, there has been a steady growth in our economic cooperation and trade volume. It is our sincere wish that we continue to work closely together to enhance our friendly relationship and ensure a sustained growth in our economic, financial and trade cooperation.

On the occasion of this reception, I wish Mr. Mayor and all our Chinese friends present here tonight good health!

Thank you!

Tasks

Task 1 Vocabulary development

Read the following words and expressions. Try to keep them in mind and find more to enrich your language bank.

A. **Useful words and expressions**

久仰大名!	I have heard a lot about you.
设宴招待	host a banquet for
谨代表	on behalf of
友好款待	gracious hospitality
贵宾	honorable guest
促进贸易	promote trade
诚挚邀请	earnest invitation
借此机会	take this opportunity
巩固友谊	strengthen the friendship
祝酒	propose a toast

知己	bosom friend
致以热烈的欢迎	extend a warm welcome
深感荣幸……	feel honored to …
不远万里来到……	come all the way to …
慢走!	Take care!
小小心意,不成敬意。	This is a token of our appreciation.
飞行时差反应	jet lag
正式邀请	official invitation
您先请。	After you!
一篇欢迎辞	a welcoming address
周到的安排	thoughtful arrangement

B. Sample sentences

| Introduction & welcoming | • I'm Li Ying from ABC Company.
• I would like to introduce the honored guests attending the party.
• Mr. Kirk, I would like to introduce you to Li Liang, the CEO of our company.
• I'm pleased to make your acquaintance.
• We've been expecting you.
• We are glad you could come.
• I welcome you on behalf of our general manager.
• Welcome to China/Nanjing/our company.
• I hope you will enjoy your stay here.
• Is this the first time that you come to China?
• How was your journey?
• Wish your visit a complete success.
• Do you have jet lag?
• It is such a delight to have friends coming from afar!
• Long distance separates no bosom friends.
• I'm sure that your present visit will strengthen the friendship between us and promote trade between our two countries. |

Expressing thanks	· Thank you very much for picking me up. · I'm deeply touched by your warm welcome. · Let me express my gratitude to Mr. Smith. · I feel honored to come here. · We'd like to assure you that we do value our long association with ABC Company. · I would like to begin by thanking Mr. White for his kind invitation. · I would like to take this opportunity to express our sincere thanks to our host for their earnest invitation and gracious hospitality we have received.
Farewell	· This trip of our American friends has been very fruitful/productive/successful. · The past seven days have been both intense and pleasant. · See you again in the near future. · I hope you'll come back to China again! · Bon voyage. · These fine impressions will forever remain in our most cherished memories. · I am looking forward to visiting your country in the near future. · I look forward to another chance to receive you in China. · I'd like to propose a toast to your health, to the continuation of our friendship and cooperation, and of course, to a pleasant journey tomorrow.

■ Task 2 Cultural salon

Read the following passage and try to get some knowledge about business protocol and etiquette.

Business protocol and etiquette in America

First meetings

American greetings are generally quite informal. This is not intended to show lack of respect, but rather a manifestation of the American belief that everyone is equal. It is expected in business situations to shake hands upon introduction, and maintain eye contact at the same time. Americans smile a lot and like to have their smiles reciprocated.

Americans view the business card as a source of information for the future and tend to exchange cards casually. There is no set ritual for exchanging business cards.

Business meetings

In a country that prides itself on its individualism, companies are organized and structured with many different styles depending on the industry, the company's history and its current leaders. In the United States, business relationships are formed between companies rather than between people. Americans do business where they get the best deal and the best service. It is not important to develop a personal relationship in order to establish a long and successful business relationship.

Americans prefer directness in communication. When Americans say "yes" or "no", they mean exactly that.

When you are doing business in the United States, it's important to be on time for meetings. Arriving late is considered rude and disrespectful. Interaction and participation is important during business meetings. If you are quiet and have nothing to say, this can be looked upon as you being unprepared and not having anything to contribute.

Meeting deadlines is taken very seriously and missing agreed deadlines is seen as irresponsible.

Names

Americans are extremely informal and call most people by their first name or nickname. However, it is a good rule of thumb to address them by their title (Mr., Mrs., Ms., Dr., etc. in general) and last name (e. g., Mr. Smith) until you are specifically told otherwise. However, as mentioned, Americans may also address you by your first name immediately after being introduced to you; this is not considered rude at all and reflects the more casual style of Americans.

Management advice when managing American employees

Differences in management culture can have a big impact on employees and company performance and a good understanding of cultural differences is imperative.

In the US, employees are delegated tasks which come with clear responsibilities and instructions from their manager. Employees are held accountable for their performance in relation to the tasks assigned to them.

As mentioned previously, Americans are direct and will always say what they mean, so as a manager you will also need to get used to this style. They do not mean to insult with their directness; they just like to get to the point and do not like to waste time. The business environment is generally fast-paced with the emphasis on "getting the job done" and moving onto the next task. As mentioned previously, business is not about getting to know the individual, but about the overall company and getting the best deal.

Achievements and success within the job role are more important than seniority. Going the extra mile above and beyond your everyday role, or using creativity to tackle an issue is something which is very important in American business culture.

Unit Two

Dinner Party

 Unit objectives

After learning this unit, you should
- be able to find ways to improve your oral skills and performance;
- master the basic words and expressions about dinner party;
- know some cultural background knowledge about dinner party.

Preparing

Ⅰ. Useful words and expressions

1. 款待
2. 美味佳肴
3. 晚宴
4. 招牌菜
5. 主菜
6. 开胃菜
7. 干杯
8. 致祝酒词
9. 软饮料
10. 就餐礼仪
11. What would you like to …?
12. taste good
13. positively full
14. on behalf of
15. to the health of …
16. enjoy your meal
17. buffet reception
18. business luncheon
19. marvelous dinner
20. hospitality and warmth

Ⅱ. Useful sentences

1. What would you like to drink?
2. Please help yourselves.
3. Thank you very much for preparing such a sumptuous banquet for us today.
4. They look really inviting.
5. I would like to propose a toast to our friends.

Situational conversations

Before dining

A: How do you do? I'm Li Ming.

B: How do you do? I'm Rob, Rob Smith.

A: Nice to meet you.

B: I've heard so much about you. Glad to meet you. How are things getting?

A: Pretty well. What about you?

B: Actually not. Our flight just arrived yesterday. We were delayed taking off,

and we encountered a lot of bad weather.

A: I'm sorry to hear that. Do you intend to stay here for a while?

B: Yes, I will stay in China for a week. It is a brief business trip.

A: I believe you will enjoy your stay here. China has many places of interest to go. And Chinese people are friendly.

B: That sounds great!

A: Dinner is ready. Let's got to the table!

B: OK.

Dining

A: What would you like to drink?

B: Some wine please.

A: Would you like some chocolate?

B: No, thanks. I'm allergic to it.

A: Here are famous Hangzhou specialties. Let me try to tell you the names first. This is Beggar's Chicken, this one is West Lake Fish in Vinegar Sauce, and that one is Dongpo Braised Pork.

B: What beautiful colors! They look really inviting!

A: They taste good. Now, please help yourself.

B: (After tasting) Oh, it's delicious.

A: Here come dumplings. They are all handmade. Please have a taste.

B: Oh, how beautiful! These are really the most beautiful desserts I have ever seen in my life!

A: They are not desserts. They are the main course.

B: I really can't believe it. They are so lovely! They taste good!

After dining

A: Do you like these dishes tonight?

B: Yes. Thank you very much for preparing such a sumptuous banquet for us today. I'm very happy to be here with many new friends.

A: I'm glad you like it.

B: I'm positively full. At this point, I should like to propose a toast to our friends, Mr. Li. I wish your company a great success. To our friendship and cooperation, bottoms up.

Oral practice

I. Talk with each other about the following questions or topics

1. Why do we entertain our clients?
2. How to invite guests to dinner?
3. What are the table manners in China and Western countries?
4. How to comment on the food?
5. As a tour guide, what is the most important thing you should do when touring?

II. Situational practice

1. Xiaowang is a secretary in the Q&Q Company. Mr. Smith, a visitor from New York, is coming for a five-day conference. Xiaowang goes to the airport to welcome him. In the evening, Xiaowang takes Mr. Smith to a Western food restaurant where Xiaowang's manager, Mr. Chen, welcomes Mr. Smith on behalf of the company.

2. David is the marketing manager of the Avon Company and he is visiting the Chinese company Q&Q for a five-day conference. At the airport, a Chinese lady, Miss Lu, receives him, takes him to the hotel to check in and talks to him about his itinerary. In the evening, David has dinner with the Chinese company's manager, Mr. Cai, in a Western food restaurant.

Complementary reading

Text A

President Gao, Distinguished Guests, Our Chinese Friends, Ladies and Gentlemen,

It is a special honor for me to have a chance to speak on behalf of all the members of our delegation. I would like to express our sincere thanks to President Gao for inviting us, and for all the hard work and thought you have given to the arrangements for our visit. We are also grateful for such a marvelous dinner tonight.

I hope that we shall all enjoy the business exchanges and friendly contact in the following days. Every member of our delegation hopes that the rate of trade between our two countries will increase in the future through our mutual efforts. And I think that only by free flow of visitors can trade develop satisfactorily.

I'm very much impressed by the hospitality and warmth with which you have received us. You must have had a very busy time making all the preparations, which deserves our sincere appreciation. We are especially thankful to you for arranging the meeting and everything that you have done on our account. I hope that Mr. Gao and other Chinese friends will be able to visit our country in the future, so that we will have the chance to return some of your kindness as a host.

Apart from business contracts, these meetings will surely help enhance the understanding and friendship between us. Well begun is half done, as we say. I hope this will pave the way for further business relations between our two countries.

In closing, I would like to invite you to join me in a toast. To the trade and friendship between us! To the health of our Chinese friends! Cheers!

Text B

People who go to a formal Western dinner party for the first time may be surprised by table manners in Western culture. Knowing them will help you make a good impression. Having good table manners means knowing, for example, how to use knives and forks, when to drink a toast and how to behave at the table. Beside your napkin you will find a small bread roll and three glasses—one for white wine, one for red wine, one for water.

There are two pairs of knives and forks on the table, forks on the left and knives on the right of the plate. When you see two spoons, the big one is for the soup and the small one is for the dessert. The knife and fork that is the closest to your plate is a little bit bigger than the one beside it. When you sit down at the

Unit Two Dinner Party

table, you can take your napkin, unfold it and put it on your lap. In China, you sometimes get a hot damp cloth to clean your face and hands, which, however, is not the custom in Western countries.

Dinner starts with a small dish, which is often called an appetizer. People pray before they start eating, and other people may keep silent for a moment. Then you can say "Enjoy your meal" to each other and everybody starts eating. For the starter, which you eat with the smaller pair, you keep the knife in your right hand and the fork in your left hand. After the starter, you will get a bowl of soup—but only one bowl of soup and never ask for a second serving. The next dish is the main course. Many westerners think the chicken breast with its tender white flesh is the best part of the bird. Some people can use their fingers when they are eating chicken or other birds, but never touch beef or other meat in bones.

It is polite to eat everything up on your plate, so don't take more food than you need. At table, you should try to speak quietly and smile a lot, but do not laugh all the time. Most westerners like soft drink if they will drive home. Many of them drink white or red wine with the food.

Tasks

■ Task 1 Vocabulary development

Read the following words and expressions. Try to keep them in mind and find more to enrich your language bank.

A. Useful words and expressions

工作午餐	working/business luncheon
晚宴	dinner party/banquet
招待会	reception
茶话会	tea party
答谢宴会	return dinner
告别宴会	farewell dinner
庆功宴	glee feast

四大菜系	four cuisines
就餐礼仪	table manners
上菜	servings
美味佳肴/特色菜/招牌菜	specialty
配菜	side dish
致祝酒词	propose a toast
客套话	polite formulas
白兰地	brandy
威士忌	whisky
鸡尾酒	cocktail
香槟酒	champagne
随量	whatever like
色、香、味	color, flavor and taste
款待	entertain
菜谱	recipe/menu
订餐	order a meal
备受青睐	enjoy/gain popularity
入席	have a seat
欢聚一堂	enjoy this happy get-together

B. Sample sentences

| Ordering dishes | • May I take your order, please?
• What is the specialty of the restaurant?
• Do you have any special meals today?
• What would you recommend?
• I prefer something spicy.
• Could you tell me how this dish is cooked?
• It's the most popular dish.
• I'll try some salad. |

Entertaining guests	• Do you like Chinese food? • Help yourself to … • Try some … • Make yourself at home. • Hope you've enjoyed yourself. • It's very kind of you to say so.
Making a toast	• Cheers! • May I propose a toast to …? • Let's raise our glasses to … • May I invite you to join me in a toast to …? • Here's to your health!

Task 2 Cultural salon

Read the following passage and try to get some knowledge about business dinners.

Dinners

After you have accepted an invitation to a dinner or a party, you should know how to be a good guest. Being a good guest in a Western country is usually very simple. If you are going to visit a friend's family, the host and hostess expect you to be yourself. That is, they expect you to act naturally. Whether you are invited to dine in a colleague's home or a restaurant, bringing your best table manners along is a good idea.

GIFT—When you are invited to someone's home, bring along a token of your appreciation. It can be as simple as a jar of homemade jam or as elaborate as a fine bottle of wine. The host/hostess will be grateful that you care about them.

CLOTHING—When you receive an invitation, ask about the style of dress. Consider the purpose or type of party and the time of day when choosing the appropriate outfit. Never wear a hat at the table or a casual sleeveless shirt. Of course, if it is a business dinner party, you should dress as formal as possible.

NAPKIN—Always place the napkin on your lap when you first sit down. Fold it so that a quarter is folded over at the top. This provides you with double protection from spills.

POSTURE—Relax and enjoy time with others. Do not rock back in the dining chair and do not prop yourself up with your elbows on the table. Placing the forearm on the table edge is okay. When cutting the food, keep your elbows close to your body. They should rest comfortably near your side.

GRACE—Wait for the host/hostess to pick up their fork before you start to eat. If it is their custom to say a prayer before eating, you should not be embarrassed.

NOISE—Turn off your cell phone until the dinner is over. Do not slurp soup or blow on hot food or beverages. Do not speak with food in your mouth. If you must blow your nose, excuse yourself from the table.

LEAVING—After the dinner or party, keep the host/hostess in the mind, and leave at an appropriate time. Do not ask for a take-home bag of food.

FOLLOW-UP—Always send a thank-you note the next day. If you cannot find the time for this, call the next day and express your appreciation.

TIP—15% of the total bill is the usual tip. However, for excellent service 20% or more is the norm.

Unit Three

Business Travel

 Unit objectives

After learning this unit, you should
- be able to find ways to improve your oral skills and performance;
- master the basic words and expressions about business travel;
- know some cultural background knowledge about business travel.

Preparing

I. Useful words and expressions

1. 机场候机楼
2. 免税店
3. 登机牌
4. 单人房
5. 登记入住
6. 身份证
7. 套房
8. 接待员
9. 客房服务
10. 货币兑换服务
11. make a reservation
12. vacant room/vacancy
13. twin beds
14. direct flight
15. check out
16. carry-on baggage
17. dead/slack/off season
18. peak/busy season
19. economy class
20. credit card

II. Useful sentences

1. I'd like to book 2 seats to London on May 5th, please.
2. Can I take this traveling bag as a carry-on?
3. I'd like to book a single room with a bath from the afternoon of October 4th to the morning of October 10th.
4. Do you have a room available on April 5th?
5. Could you tell me what the economic class fare is?

Situational conversations

Booking airline tickets

A: Good morning. Can I help you?
B: Yes. I'd like to book 2 seats to London on May 5th, please.
A: Just a moment, I'll check the schedule.
B: I prefer a morning flight.
A: The only flight available is Eastern Airlines 221, which leaves at 8:30 a.m.

B: Could you tell me what the economic class fare is?
A: It's $680 one way.
B: Is it a direct flight?
A: Yes, it's a non-stop.
B: What time does it arrive in London?
A: It arrives at 6:30 p.m.
B: Fine. Book it for me, please.
A: Certainly, madam. May I have your name and telephone number?
B: Of course. Lin Fang. 66478215.
A: Thank you.

Checking in at the airport

A: May I help you, sir?
B: Yes. We're here to check in for the flight to Sydney. Here are our tickets and passports.
A: Thank you, sir. Please put your baggage on the scale. How many pieces of baggage do you want to check?
B: Twenty pieces altogether. Can I take this traveling bag as a carry-on?
A: I'm afraid not. It's overweight. The allowance for the carry-on baggage is 8 kilogram.
B: I see.
A: Here are twenty claim tags for your baggage and your passports.
B: Thank you very much.

Getting aboard a flight

A: Good morning. Welcome aboard. This way, please.
B: Thank you, stewardess. Can you direct me to my seat?
A: Certainly, may I see your boarding pass, please?
B: Sure, here it is.
A: It's 32-B. Just over there, sir.
B: Thank you, Miss. Where can I put my bag?

A: You can put your coat and small things on the tack over your head and your bag here at your feet.

B: Can I put my bag in this empty seat beside me?

A: I'm sorry. All carry-on luggage must be placed underneath the seat in front of you or in the overhead compartment.

B: Where is the button that controls my chair?

A: Right here on the arm rest.

B: Thank you.

Making a reservation

A: Advance reservations. Can I help you?

B: Yes. I'd like to book a single room with a bath from the afternoon of October 4th to the morning of October 10th.

A: Yes, we do have a single room available for those dates.

B: What is the rate, please?

A: The current rate is $50 per night.

B: What services come with that?

A: For $50 you'll have a radio, a color television, a telephone and a computer.

B: That sounds not bad at all. I'll take it.

A: Very good. Could you please tell me your name, sir?

B: Yes, it's Kirk.

A: How do you spell it, please?

B: It's K-I-R-K.

A: K-I-R-K.

B: That's right.

A: What is your telephone number?

B: (601) 264-9716. By the way, I'd like a quiet room away from the street if that is possible.

A: A quiet room away from the street is preferred. OK. We'll mail you a reservation card confirming your booking as soon as possible. We look forward to your visit.

B: Thank you and goodbye.
A: Goodbye.

Checking in

A: Good afternoon, sir. Is there anything I can do for you?
B: Yes, my name is Jim Kirk. I'm from Britain. The day before yesterday, my secretary in Hong Kong booked a single room for me in this hotel.
A: Just one moment, please. I'll check up.
(*Checking the reservation list*)
A: Yes, there it is. Jim Kirk of British Petroleum, Hong Kong branch. A single room for seven days, right?
B: Right. What's the room number?
A: Room 909. Could you fill in this form, please? I'll also need your passport.
B: Here you are.
A: Could you sign your name here, please?
B: All right.
A: Thank you. Here is your key card. You can find all the information about this hotel from the information card in your room. The bellboy will take you to your room.
B: Thank you. By the way, where can I change money?
A: At the change counter on the right hand of this lobby.
B: Thank you very much for your help.
A: You are welcome.

Checking out

A: Good morning. May I help you?
B: Yes, I'd like to check out now. My name is Jim Kirk, Room 909. Here's the key card.
A: One moment, please, sir. Here's your bill. Would you like to check and see if the amount is correct?
B: What's the 15 dollars for?

A: That's for the phone calls you made from your room.

B: Can I pay with the traveler's cheque?

A: Certainly. May I have your passport, please?

B: Here you are.

A: Could you sign each cheque here for me?

B: Sure.

A: Here are your receipt and your change, sir. Thank you.

B: Thank you. Goodbye.

Oral practice

I. Talk with each other about the following questions or topics

1. What are the reasons for a business trip?
2. What would you pack for your business trip?
3. What is important when choosing accommodations for a business trip?
4. What may cause you stress during your business trip?

II. Situational practice

1. You are on a business trip and you want to stay an extra day. Telephone the airline office to arrange a different flight.

2. Telephone Rainbow Holiday Inn to book a single room for 5 days from May 11th to 15th.

3. Jim is a clerk of ABC Company. He has just finished a business talk with Mr. White. Jim suggests a round-city tour with Mr. White and he volunteers to be the guide. So the two make a practical arrangement and decide to begin their excursion at 8:00 a.m. the next morning.

Complementary reading

Text A

Business travel refers to any type of geographical transportation that someone undergoes at the behest of his or her employer to perform the duties of a job. One simple way in which an employee may undergo such travel is for training, in which an employer may require that employees go to a central location to receive instruction. Business travel can also include ongoing and regular visit to various locations in order to provide services or otherwise work with remote teams. This type of travel is always temporary, as the employee eventually returns home, as opposed to "relocation" that is typically permanent.

 The purpose of business travel can vary quite a bit, depending on the particular needs of an employer and the types of skills possessed by a traveler. Training, for example, is a common cause for this type of travel as employees may need to go to a central office or similar location to be trained. Developments in computers and training software have alleviated the need for such travel in many fields, though some companies may still require training in person.

 There are also many situations in which an employee working in sales may need to travel for his or her employer. This can be a fairly short trip, such as someone driving across town to meet with a client and pitch a sale in person rather than over the phone. More extensive business travel may be required in some situations, however, such as flights to other cities or countries. Some companies may need certain employees to travel extensively to work with individuals in other offices, often providing training or services to assist those locations.

 Businesses typically reimburse employees for business travel, or provide them with funds in advance to cover travel costs. An employee who has to drive to a sales pitch, for example, may be reimbursed by an employer for the cost of the gas used in doing so. Airline tickets are often purchased for employees by a company, and the costs for hotel rooms and food while traveling are typically provided. Additional travel expenses may also be covered, especially for charges that are made as part of an employee's work.

 Although business travel involves the transportation of an employee from one place to another, it should not be confused with relocation. When an employee travels somewhere for a company, it is typically expected that he or she will return home after a fairly short period of time. Extensive travel may be necessary in some situations, but it is still temporary. Relocation, however, occurs when an employee completely moves to a new area at the behest of a company, often due to a promotion or recent hiring.

Text B

(*Mr. Jacques Lepac arrives from Paris to Chicago*)

CBP(Customs and Border Patrol) Officer: Welcome to the United States. Can I see your I-94 form, please?

Mr. Lepac: I'm sorry, my what?

CBP Officer: Your I-94 form. It's the white arrival/departure form a flight attendant gave you on the plane.

Mr. Lepac: Oh, yes, the one with my name and the address of where I'm staying in the U.S. (Hands it to CBP Officer)

CBP Officer: Why are you visiting the United States, Mr. Lepac?

Mr. Lepac: On business.

CBP Officer: What type of business are you in?

Mr. Lepac: I'm in sales. I sell computers.

CBP Officer: Do you have any documentation from your company?

Mr. Lepac: Yes, here is my business card.

CBP Officer: What will you be doing in the United States, Mr. Lepac?

Mr. Lepac: I'm attending a company meeting at our office in downtown Chicago.

CBP Officer: How long will you be here?

Mr. Lepac: One week. I'll be participating in meetings through Friday and then will catch up with a friend for the weekend. I will return to France on Sunday.

CBP Officer: I see. Where will you be staying while you're in the country?

Mr. Lepac: I'll be at the New Continental Hotel.

CBP Officer: Have you been to the United States before?

Mr. Lepac: No, this is my first trip to this country.

CBP Officer: Can I see your passport, please?

Mr. Lepac: Sure. I have my passport right here.
CBP Officer: I'll stamp that for you. I'll also need to see your customs declaration form.
Mr. Lepac: I don't have anything to declare. I haven't brought anything other than my clothes with me.
CBP Officer: All of your paperwork is in order, Mr. Lepac. Keep your documents with you at all times. Have a good visit.
Mr. Lepac: Thank you.

Tasks

Task 1 Vocabulary development

Read the following words and expressions. Try to keep them in mind and find more to enrich your language bank.

A. Useful words and expressions

旅行计划	itinerary
起飞时间	departure time
机场大楼	terminal building
问讯处	information desk
安全检查	security check
旅行/居留签证	travel/residence visa
签证有效期	validity of visa
商务舱	business class
海关	the Customs
关税	customs duty
免税/应税商品	duty-free/dutiable goods/articles
行李提取处	baggage/luggage claim
豪华套房	luxury suite
单人房	single room
双人房	twin-bedded room

空调	air-conditioner
唤醒服务	morning call/wake-up call service
商务中心	business center
健身房	gym
洗衣服务	laundry service
窗户朝南的房间	room with windows facing south
有大阳台的房间	room with a large balcony
寄存行李	deposit one's luggage
团队预订折扣	discount for group reservation
旅行支票	traveler's cheque
报销	reimburse

B. Sample sentences

At the airport	• I'd like to know whether there is a flight to Frankfurt. • Is there a non-stop flight to Beijing? • Where can I get my boarding pass and have my luggage weighed? • Can I have my luggage checked here for the flight to Bangkok? • What's the departure time of the flight? • Is the plane on schedule? • Can I take this as a carry-on? • Can I have a seat in the back of the plane?
Making a reservation	• I'd like to know if you have vacant rooms for us. • I'd like to reserve a double room for two nights. • The suites are too expensive. A single room is okay. • I will arrive late but please keep my reservation.
Specific requirements	• I'd like a single/double room with a bath. • I want to have a corner room with windows facing south. • I'd like a room with a very large bed. • I'd like a room with a very large balcony. • Could I have a room with two single beds?

Services	· May I have room service/cleaning service/laundry service, please? · Here is something wrong with the TV. Would you get it fixed, please? · How can I access WiFi in my room? · May I have a morning call at 7 o'clock tomorrow morning, please? · Are there any Chinese TV channels in the room? · May I check out and deposit my luggage here?
Prices	· What is the price difference between a single room and a twin-bedded room? · Does the price include breakfast? · How much is a suite for two nights? · Is there a discount/reduction for group reservation? · Do we have to pay a full price for children?

■ Task 2 Cultural salon

Read the following passage and try to get some knowledge about business trips.

Tips for a stress-free business trip

Business trips aren't always easy, especially if you are traveling a lot. Your employer generally expects a lot from you within a short amount of time. Also, change of weather, less sleep and eating outside can disrupt your routine and as a result, decrease your health. Below you can find some tips for a stress-free business trip.

Keep healthy snacks in your carry-on

If possible, eat well before you board the plane. The food on the flight may not be healthy and can upset your stomach. If you don't have the time to eat before your flight, eat the snacks you have in your carry-on bag. When you arrive at your destination, assuming that you don't know the city, it may not be easy for you to find a restaurant for your taste. Keep some pills/vitamins with you as well.

Join a reward program

Join an airline or a travel/hotel reward program and stick with it. Use your points to upgrade yourself to a better room or first-class compartment. Also, loyal members of reward programs usually have privileges like priority over boarding or free same day flight change. Another key point is to check in to your flight online so you can skip the long lines at the airport.

Don't check your luggage

If you are going for a day or two, use a carry-on bag. This will both save you time when you land and eliminate the risk of losing your luggage when you transfer flights. If you need to check your luggage, at least pack spare clothes. In this case, you have a backup plan to fall back on. Moreover, don't forget to check the weather before you pack your suitcase.

Charge everything

Charge all of your electronics before your flight. Keep travel chargers with you in case you run out of battery. You never know if you will need your laptop during flight to work or immediately after flight for a meeting. Also, you may need to use map/GPS applications from your cell phone when you arrive at your destination. Therefore, you should always be prepared in advance.

Relax and enjoy your time

If possible, do not sit with your coworkers during flight so you can avoid talking about work. Sit back and listen to some music, eat your sandwich or take a nap. Use this time to charge yourself and get ready for your landing. Don't forget you are in a new city, so do some sightseeing—if you have any spare time.

Unit Four Business Interview  33

Unit Four

Business Interview

 Unit objectives

After learning this unit, you should
- find ways to improve your presentation skills in business interviews;
- master the basic words and expressions about business interviews;
- know common practice and etiquette in business interviews.

Preparing

Ⅰ. Useful words and expressions

1. 助手
2. 试用期
3. 深度访谈
4. 单身的
5. 已婚的
6. 应邀
7. 出生地
8. 出生日期
9. 业余爱好
10. 工作经历
11. personality
12. C. V.
13. major
14. by appointment
15. current affairs
16. two-year gap
17. career plan
18. marketing management
19. apprentice
20. headline

Ⅱ. Useful sentences

1. How would you describe yourself?
2. State your unique selling proposition.
3. I will work with and support whoever might get selected.
4. I am motivated by targets.
5. I really enjoy being part of a team.

Situational conversations

Interview opening

A: I have come here for the interview for administrative assistant by appointment. Nice to meet you.

B: Nice to meet you, too. Please be seated.

A: Thank you!

B: What is your name, please?

A: My name is Sun Li.

B: What is your greatest strength?
A: Well, I approach things very enthusiastically, I think, and I don't like to leave things half-done. I'm very organized and extremely capable.

Character

A: What kind of character do you think you have?
B: Generally speaking, I am an open-minded person.
A: What is your greatest strength?
B: Cheerfulness and friendliness.
A: What's your friends' or colleagues' impression of you?
B: They say Mr. Sun is a friendly, sensitive, caring and determined person.
A: What kind of personality do you admire?
B: I admire a person who is honest, flexible and easy-going.
A: How do you get along with others?
B: I get on well with others.

Personal information

A: Mr. Sun, would you mind if I ask you any questions which may sound impolite?
B: Ah, never mind, please.
A: Can you tell me how old you are?
B: I am 25 years old.
A: Are you married?
B: No, I am still single.
A: Can you tell me any things about your family?
B: OK. There are four persons in my family, my parents, my elder sister and me.

Educational background

A: Which university did you graduate from?
B: I graduated from JS University.
A: What subject did you major in at university?

B: I majored in Economics.

A: Tell me about the courses of your major at university.

B: I took more than 50 courses at university, including Microeconomics, Macroeconomics, Marketing Principles, Sales Management, Statistics and so on.

A: How did you get on with your studies at university?

B: I did well at university. I was one of the top students in the class.

A: What subject did you minor in?

B: I didn't minor in any subject when I was at university, but I attended English and computer courses. And I am currently studying finance in a training school.

Work goal

A: Could you project what you would like to be doing five years from now?

B: As I have some administrative experience from my last job, I may use my organizational and planning skills in the future.

A: How do you plan to accomplish this?

B: By doing everything necessary and further study.

A: How long would you like to stay with this company?

B: How long I will stay with the company depends on whether the company and I are satisfied with each other.

A: What do you think of the outlook of this industry in five years?

B: I do believe this industry will develop rapidly in 5 years' time.

Oral practice

I. Talk with each other about the following questions or topics

1. How to introduce yourself to the interviewer?
2. How to design your future work plan?
3. How to deal with the conflicts presented by the interviewer?
4. How to tell the interviewer about your approach to a project?

II. Situational practice

1. The interviewer wants you to talk about your approaches to dealing with conflicts between managers and stakeholders. Working with difficult stakeholders is one of those areas where your transferable soft skills are extremely important. They want you to have a bit of insight into the challenges you might face at this organization.

2. When you're competing for an internal position within your company, you may be asked what you will do if you don't get the job. The interviewer wants to know whether you are concerned about just the advancement opportunity or the company. Try to think about what the interviewers are looking for and keep this in mind as you answer questions of this kind.

3. Interviewers want you to talk about your own strengths and weaknesses. This kind of common job interview questions can be asked in many different ways. Strengths should be easy enough to think about. Talking about weaknesses can be harder but good interview answers are still possible. Please talk about your answers.

Complementary reading

Text A

Job interview

An interview is an important event in a job-hunting process, because the 20 or 30 minutes you spend with the interviewer may decide whether or not you get the particular job you want. Therefore, it is important to remember that your purpose during an interview may differ from that of the potential employer. You want to make yourself stand out as a whole person who has personal strengths and should be considered the right person for the job. It is encouraging to know that the interviewer's task is not to embarrass you, but to hire the right person for the job.

Remember, the job hunting is very competitive. Anything you can do to

improve your interview techniques will be to your advantage. The following suggestions may help you land the most important job.

Your goal in an interview is to make sure your good points get across. The interviewer won't know them unless you point them out, so try to do this in a factual and sincere manner.

Don't say anything bad about your former employers. If you have been fired from a job and the interviewer asks about it, be honest.

Show the interviewer that you are interested in the company by asking questions. Ask about responsibilities, working conditions, promotion opportunities and benefits of the job you are applying for.

If at some point you decide the interview is not going well, do not let your discouragement show. You have nothing to lose by continuing a show of confidence, and you may have much to gain. It may be real, or it may be a test to see how you react to adverse conditions.

Some interviewers may bring up the salary early in the interview. At this time, you may indicate that you are more interested in a job where you can prove yourself than a specific salary. This politely passes the question back to the interviewer. If possible, you should negotiate for the salary after you have been offered a job and have completed the paperwork.

Text B

(A = Manager, B = Wilson)

A: Can you tell me a little bit about yourself?

B: I am a graduate of a technical university and have been employed as a technician with ABC Company for approximately 10 years.

A: Please explain why you are leaving your current position and please elaborate on your technical skills.

B: I am looking for a growth opportunity, which I feel is not available at my current position. In terms of skills, I am Microsoft certified in Windows XP and several other operating systems.

Unit Four Business Interview

A: Where do you see yourself five years from now?

B: I see myself in a management position.

A: I've just looked over your resume and I must admit I am quite impressed.

B: Thank you. I've worked pretty hard to be able to list those accomplishments.

A: You've got plenty of training and experience. I wonder if you could tell me something about your goals. Where do you see yourself ten years from now?

B: To be honest, I don't plan in that much detail. My goals tend to be general; I define success according to the job at hand. I see myself advancing as I succeed, but I don't necessarily dwell on the timing of each step.

A: Interesting! And how do you feel about decision-making? Are you an independent thinker, or do you depend more on your superior for direction?

B: That depends a bit on the problem at hand. There are certain situations in which a manager can give a general directive, and expect his employees to know how to take the initiative on the details. I am known for taking the initiative, but I believe I also have the discernment to wait for direction when the situation calls for that.

Tasks

■ Task 1 Vocabulary development

Read the following words and expressions. Try to keep them in mind and find more to enrich your language bank.

A. Useful words and expressions

应约	by appointment
副经理	assistant manager
离职	quit a job
紧密跟随行业发展	keep up with the development of the industry
有效率的	efficient

学士	bachelor
奖学金	scholarship
辅修	minor
资格	qualification
不具有挑战性	of no challenge
晋升	advancement
背景	background
代表处	representative office
推荐信	recommendation
协调员	coordinator
工作经历	occupational history
目标明确的	goal-oriented
自我发展	self-remould
期待薪水	salary expectation
奖金	bonus
通讯记者	correspondent
日程安排表	schedule
通知	notify
和……取得联系	get in touch with …

B. Sample sentences

Basic expressions	· May I come in? · How are you doing, Mrs. Smith? · Excuse me, may I see Mrs. Smith? · Will you come in, please? Take a seat. · I have come here for an interview by appointment. Nice to meet you. · Did you have any difficulty finding our company? · How do you think of the weather today? · I am familiar with this area.

Personal information	· What is your name, please? · Can you tell me what your full name is, please? · I was born on June 22, 1980. · You look very young. How old are you? · Where is your native place? · Where do you live now?
Characters	· What kind of character do you think you have? · Are you introverted or extroverted? · What kind of person would you like to work with? · I get on well with others. · I have an interest in traveling.
Educational backgrounds	· What degree will you receive? · I will receive a Bachelor's degree. · How about your academic records in college? · I have been doing quite well in college. · My specialization at university is just in line with the areas your institute deals with. · My major is Business Administration.
Personal techniques	· How do you think of your English? · I think my English is good enough to communicate with English-speaking people. · Have you obtained any certificates of technical qualifications? · What special skills do you have? Can you tell me? · I have received an Engineer Qualification Certificate. · What other foreign language do you speak? · I am accomplished in programming.
Working goals	· Are you a goal-oriented person? · What is your long-range objective? · I do believe this industry will develop rapidly in 5 years' time.

Task 2 Cultural salon

Read the following passage and try to get some knowledge about business interview.

Tips for business interview

Business interview is very important for many graduates. Some job interviewers ask tough questions to trip you up or to get you to reveal information you may be trying to conceal. Others want to get a better sense of your thought process or see how you respond under pressure. Whatever the reason, you'll want to be prepared. Here are some useful tips for you.

Tip 1

Don't discuss your goals for returning to school or having a family. They are not relevant and could knock you out of contention for a job. Rather, you want to connect your answer to the job you are applying for.

Tip 2

You walk into the interview room, shake hands with your interviewer and sit down with your best interviewing smile on. Guess what their first question is? "Tell me about yourself." Your interviewer is not looking for a 10-minute dissertation here. Instead, offer one razor sharp sentence or two that sets the stage for further discussion and sets you apart from your competitors.

Tip 3

Give them "your synopsis of you" answer, specifically your unique selling proposition. What a difference you've made with this statement! Your interviewer is now sitting forward in her chair giving you her full attention. At this point, you might add the following sentence: "I'd like to discuss how I might be able to do something like that for you." The ball is now back in her court and you have the beginnings of a real discussion and not an interrogation process.

Tip 4

Try to think about what the interviewers are looking for and keep this in mind as you answer interview questions. Remember the job advert? Were they looking

for initiative, a good communicator, someone with good attention to detail? Describe yourself in these terms. Start with "I am ..." and not with "I think ..." or "I believe ..." so that you sound self-aware and confident.

Tip 5

Sometimes, interviewers want to know about your ability. As a result, they will ask you to talk about your strengths and weaknesses. This common job interview question can be asked in many different ways, such as "What qualities do you admire in others that you would like to develop in yourself?"

Talking about weaknesses can be harder but good interview answers are still possible. Many people choose to mention something which they've recognized as being a weakness but have overcome. On a final note, it's much safer to highlight your lack of experience or knowledge as a weakness than a fault in your personality. Employers can always give you experience but few want to help you overcome shortcomings in your personality! So avoid telling interviewers that you "get bored" or "too involved" or "frustrated"!

Tip 6

If the interviewers focus on other pressure, such as pressure to meet targets, dealing with difficult customers etc, give an appropriate reply, and mention past situations where you have coped under such pressure. For example, you can say "I know that all jobs involve some sort of pressure at some time. I can work as well under pressure as I do at any other time but when I am busy, I prioritize activities so that my workload is manageable".

Unit Five

Business Presentation

 Unit objectives

After learning this unit, you should
- find ways to improve your oral skills and performance;
- master the basic words and expressions about business presentation;
- know some cultural background knowledge of business presentation.

Unit Five Business Presentation

Preparing

I. Useful words and expressions

1. 屏幕
2. 图表
3. 受邀参会
4. 营销方式
5. 市场调研
6. 按照下列次序
7. 接受一个订单
8. 质量监控
9. 总而言之
10. 分享观点
11. commodity features
12. sequence
13. order
14. monopoly
15. run out of time
16. profit
17. manufacturing industry
18. service industry
19. operation
20. degree of customer satisfaction

II. Useful sentences

1. I would like to present our comments in the following order.

2. First of all, I will outline the characteristics of our product.

3. If you are interested, I will prepare a list of them.

4. By the way, before leaving this subject, I would like to add a few comments.

5. To finish my presentation, our company will be very happy to receive your order at any time.

Situational conversations

Feelings about presentation

A: Hi, Tony, this is Jenny. How are you doing?

B: I've just returned from the Head Office. The weather is great! Beijing is a great city!

A: Have you met John yet?

B: No, I haven't seen him yet. We have a meeting at 10 o'clock tomorrow morning. We are going to meet then.

A: Have you made your presentation yet?

B: Yes, I made the presentation yesterday evening. I was very nervous, but everything went well.

A: Has management given you any feedback yet?

B: Yes, I've already met with the sales director. We met immediately after the meeting and he was impressed with our work.

A: That's great, Tony. Congratulations! Have you visited any museums yet?

B: No, I'm afraid I haven't had any time yet. I hope to take a tour around town tomorrow.

A: Well, I'm happy to hear that everything is going well. I'll talk to you soon.

B: Thanks for calling, Jenny. Bye.

A: Bye.

Practicing a presentation

A: Betty, can I run your new presentation?

B: Certainly, I'd love to hear some of the new concepts.

A: OK, here goes ... On behalf of myself and Sport Outfitters, I'd like to welcome you. My name's Jim Smith. This morning, I'd like to outline our new campaign concepts that have been recently developed.

B: Excuse me, who was invited to this conference?

A: Our sales representatives from our branch offices were asked to come. I think a number of upper-management representatives were also invited.

B: That's good. Our marketing approach is going to be completely revamped.

A: And that's why we need everyone to be informed. So, I'll continue. You'll be given the background and I'll talk you through the results of some of our recent market studies.

B: How many surveys were completed?

A: I think about 100,000 were returned to the company. Our marketing team was very pleased with the response.

Unit Five Business Presentation

B: OK, continue ...

A: The presentation has been divided into three parts. Firstly, our past approach. Secondly, changes that will be made. Thirdly, future forecasts ...

B: That sounds good.

A: If you have any questions, please don't hesitate to ask. At the end of this presentation, a short advertisement will be shown to give you an idea of where we are going.

B: Good job, Jim. I hope your graphics are being put together by Carter.

A: Of course they are. You know he's the best!

Oral practice

Sample script for opening and closing your presentation

I. Here is a sample script for use in planning your opening remarks

1. "Good evening! My name is (name) and this is (name), (name), (name), and (name). We are from the (organization)."

2. "We're here this evening to talk to you about a business issue that we feel is of great importance."

3. "Our objective is not to try and persuade you to take a stand on this issue, but we would like to try and present both sides of the issue to you in order to better educate the public on a very important business concern."

4. "We want to take this opportunity to thank you for allowing us to come before the (name of the organization) for this Business Issues Forum. Our topic today is: (title of the business issue being presented)."

(The opening remarks may be made by the teacher or the leader of the group making the presentation.)

From this point, you'll want to begin introducing the business issue. From a verbal analysis, the listeners should not be able to tell whether the presenter is for or against the issue. Use the presentation steps to analyze your presentation to avoid letting the listeners determine if the presenter is for or against the issue.

II. Here is a sample script for use in closing your presentation

1. "As we bring our Business Issues Forum to a close, we once again thank you for allowing us to be here this evening and hope that this activity has given you a much clearer understanding of (restate the business issue which was presented)."

2. "We would welcome the opportunity to return with another group of students to present a different Business Issues Forum topic in the near future."

Topics for discussion

1. What is a business presentation? Why do people present?
2. What are the types of a business presentation in terms of the purpose?
3. How can a business presentation be clearly organized?
4. What are the features of an effective business presentation?
5. What techniques can be applied to make a good business presentation?
6. What's the Five-step Approach in making an effective business presentation?

Complementary reading

A leader is only as good as his presentation skills
By Julie Hill

No matter the company, the people at the top are different—sort of. Their skills, knowledge, and talents have put them in positions to lead and inspire, but that doesn't mean they can or will. Although senior managers usually get a hefty salary, a nice office, and a competent staff, they aren't immune to the most common challenges of presenting: anxiety, lack of preparation time, nervous tics, off-message rambling, and misreading an audience.

Overcoming hindrances. Still, many top executives slog through their day-to-day duties without paying much attention to their presentation skills, and in the process, sometimes set themselves up for failure or disappointment. Those who work in the cottage industry of executive coaching say that one of the most insidious obstacles to presentation improvement at this level is a lack of self-awareness borne of the very success that brought an executive to the top.

According to Merna Skinner, a partner and consultant at Exec/Comm, "Many executives say, 'I know my business and I know my content, just put some words in front of me and I'll be fine.' In reality, it's rare to meet an individual who can do presentations cold and still deliver."

Jeary recently wrote a book, *Speaking from the Top*, aimed at senior executives who need to hone their presentation skills. Among the many challenges Jeary addresses is the executive's need for a team of individuals to rely on not only to design slides and make sure the Teleprompter works, but also to research who's in the audience. "There could be vendors from the outside, internal staff, stockholders, the media. There could be analysts, or employees from a sister company," he points out.

Comfort level. Giuliano counsels clients to speak to the audience's needs rather than their own. The trap executives get into too often is that their presentation is delivered from the speaker's perspective of what the audience needs to know. "As a result," Giuliano says, "it doesn't speak to audience members' comfort level, their fears, their objectives, their emotional states. So it's important to frame the message for the audience."

To find this elusive comfort level, Giuliano advises developing a network of people with different points of view who can provide valuable clues about what a given audience is thinking. "This network feeds us with what people are feeling, so the speaker can address those things, actually bringing these people into the communication process." Inside a company, this form of networking can be as easy as maintaining regular contact with employees at all levels; outside one's own company, however, it requires some initiative on the speaker's part to contact people who will be in the audience.

Peter Giuliano's networking principles and Tony Jeary's team strategies do more than address audience issues. They impress upon executives that important speeches are not projects they should tackle alone. When it comes to key presentations, there is no shame in asking for help.

According to Giuliano, the first line of defense for anxiety is the one some executives fight the most—rehearsal. "Many resist the need to rehearse, under the foolish notion that it will sound fresh if they don't. Instead, it just opens them up for unknown possibilities."

Failure isn't an option. Exec/Comm's Merna Skinner also stresses the need for executives to rehearse. "Practice helps presenters feel more comfortable with the visual mechanics and other pieces of the presentation," she says.

Skinner advises her clients to do three types of practices. The first should get the presenter used to reading the words with the medium he will use to present, be it a script, teleprompter or scrolling screen. This allows the executive to find out if his words feel natural. The second time through is to practice for pausing, pacing and punching the correct words. The final run-through should be practiced in the presentation's venue. This allows the presenter to familiarize himself with where he will stand, what the room looks like and how the multimedia or AV equipment will work.

On the whole, the obstacles executive presenters face aren't too different from the challenges facing presenters at all levels of an organization. The primary difference is that the privilege of being a big cheese comes with inflated expectations, more pressure and higher risks. Failure isn't—or shouldn't be—an option.

In short, when it comes to presentation skills, the biggest difference between top executives and everyone else is that they have no excuse. Every organization has its share of top executives, but there's no reason their presentations have to stink. With a little humility and help, every executive presentation can be a resounding success.

Unit Five Business Presentation

Tasks

Task 1 Vocabulary development

Read the following words and expressions. Try to keep them in mind and find more to enrich your language bank.

A. Useful words and expressions

hefty	数额巨大的
tic	抽筋
rambling	杂乱无章的
hindrance	妨碍
slog	努力苦干
cottage industry	家庭手工业
insidious	潜在的,阴险的
hone	磨炼
Teleprompter	讲词提示器
elusive	逃避的
scrolling screen	滚动屏幕
punch	用重音读出
run-through	从头到尾读一遍
a big cheese	大人物
stink	惹人讨厌
humility	谦逊
resounding	令人瞩目的
impromptu	即兴的
extemporaneous	即席的
spontaneously	自发地
manuscript	手稿
bookish	书生气的
panicking	慌乱的

bar chart	柱状图
digress	离题
flowchart	流程图
graph	（曲线）图表
mind map	思维导图
monologue	独白
multimedia	多媒体
pie chart	饼分图
poster	海报
slide projector	幻灯机

B. Sample sentences

Starting the presentation	• Good morning/Good afternoon, ladies and gentlemen. • I'd like to thank you all for coming here today. • First of all, I'd like to introduce myself.
Stating the topic or purpose	• The topic of my presentation today is … • What I'm going to talk about today is … • The purpose of my talk is to give you some information about … • I'd like to give you a brief presentation about …

Stating the structure	• I'd like to take you through today's presentation briefly.
	• I've divided my talk into three parts.
	• The structure of my talk will be as follows: firstly, the history, then, the markets, and lastly, the staff.
	• The main points I will be talking about are …
	    firstly …
	    secondly …
	    next … finally …

Mentioning time constraints, visual aids or questions	• My presentation will last for about fifteen minutes and I'll be using the PowerPoint. • Please feel free to interrupt me with any questions you may have during the presentation. • I'd like to ask you to keep any questions you may have to the end of the presentation.

Introducing the first point	· Let's start/begin with ...
Showing graphics, transparencies, slides, etc.	· I'd like to illustrate this by showing you ... · This point can be made more clearly in this chart. · As you can see from this graph, sales picked up dramatically last year. · The dotted line represents sales for the year before last.
Moving on to the next point	· Now let's move on to ... · After that, we'll be taking a look at ...
Giving more details	· I'd like to expand on this aspect/problem/point. · Would you like me to expand on/elaborate on that? · As far as this point is concerned, I need to talk about it in detail. · To illustrate this, I have an example for you.
Changing to a different topic	· So much for .... /This is all I want to say about this point. · I'd like to turn to something completely different.
Referring to something which is off the topic	· I'd like to digress here for a moment and just mention that ...
Referring back to an earlier point	· Let me go back to what I said earlier about ...

Summarizing or concluding	· I'd like to recap/summarize the main points of my presentation.
	    —first we covered ...
	    —then we talked about ...
	    —finally we looked at ...
	· I'm going to conclude by saying that/inviting you to/ quoting ...

Questions	· Finally, I'll be happy to answer your questions if you have any now. · Now I'd like to invite any questions you may have. · That's a tricky question. · Thank you for your question.

Task 2 Cultural salon

Read the following passage and try to get some knowledge about business presentations.

10 ways to give a kickass business presentation

Business presentations don't have to all be the same, and being in the audience during one doesn't have to be sleep-inducing. It is possible to make every business presentation entertaining, informative and enjoyable for all parties involved.

Experts shared their best tips for creating and giving a killer presentation that will engage your audience and help you land the sale.

1. Include only the necessary information.

"A good business presentation ... has one main point and everything is structured around that point. It doesn't rely heavily upon PowerPoint or slides filled with text, and it allows time for discussion and asking questions."—Eddie Rice, speechwriter at Custom Speech Writing

2. Lead with your main point.

"No secret sauce, tech or gimmicks. What makes any presentation engaging and effective is to put the bottom line up front and then provide whatever backup data may be needed. I've seen many presentations where the story is dragged out and tension is built, as if the person was trying to make a movie. But ... people are busy and need to deal with the issue and then move on."—Mark McMillion, principal at McMillion Leadership Associates LLC

3. Let yourself, not your slides, shine.

"Focus more on what you will say and how you will say it rather than on having the coolest slides. Not everything you say should be on your slides. No more than three sentences per slide. Present your best data, or no data at all—but not all your data."—Michael Ann Strahilevitz, PhD, visiting scholar, Duke University

4. Tailor your presentation to the audience.

"The true meaning of the presentation is to engage with people and persuade them to your point of view, not just deliver chunks of information. Every presentation, no matter the subject, must be tailored specifically to the people you are talking to. If you tell an anecdote, don't simply repeat the same story wherever you are—not only will it become stale, you'll also fail to make a connection to the people you're addressing."—Stuart Ross, founder, High Growth

5. Rehearse beforehand.

"What makes a good business presentation is practice, practice, practice! It's just like sports. You have to repeatedly practice your presentation to improve it."
—Andrew J. Zurbuch, broker/owner at Integrated Financial Solutions Inc.

6. Let your personality show.

"Authenticity is engaging. Too many presentations are technically proficient but lack heart. If you are not genuine, there will be an unbridgeable gap between you and your listeners. Authenticity is the most important element of an effective communication in any context."—Brandt Johnson, principal at Syntaxis Inc.

7. Keep your energy up.

"A high energy level is the most important step to take in presentations. This applies to any type of speaking, any size of audience and any topic. If you seemed bored or tired, that vibe will translate to your audience."—Ken Boyd, co-founder & chief educator, AccountingEd.com

8. Use "bridges" when going from topic to topic.

"Some ways to create great segues include bridge words, such as 'furthermore', 'meanwhile', 'however', 'consequently' and 'finally'; bridge phrases, such as 'in addition to', 'a similar example is', 'do you remember when I said', 'on the other hand' and 'in conjunction with'; and bridge actions, such as asking the audience questions, going point by point, using visual aids, pausing and physical movements."—Parker Geiger, CEO, CHUVA group

9. Use body language to connect with your audience.

"Dynamic presenters use their hands, facial expressions, and eye contacts to keep the audience engaged. If possible, use props and stage movements to keep the audience interested."—Matt Reischer, founder, Legal Advice

10. Keep it simple.

"Simple explanations coupled with simple graphics equal one amazing presentation. People think you need to jam a bunch of data in the slides, but it's a huge mistake. Pick specific points to talk about and create simple graphics to reinforce the point. Do not give the viewer extra information."—Gary Tuch, co-founder, professor of Egghead Science Academy

Unit Six

Enterprise Introduction

 Unit objectives

After learning this unit, you should
- understand the tactics and processes of enterprise introduction;
- master the basic words and expressions about enterprise introduction;
- know some cultural background knowledge about enterprise introduction.

Preparing

Ⅰ. Useful words and expressions

1. 商标
2. 工厂设施
3. 客户经理
4. 收购的公司
5. 服务类型
6. 企业管理
7. 增值
8. 广告业
9. 售后服务
10. 代理人
11. amalgamation
12. analyst
13. bankruptcy
14. Board of Directors
15. fair average quality
16. financial ability
17. financial report
18. fixed cost
19. handicraft industry
20. holding company

Ⅱ. Useful sentences

1. This corporation is a leading global information technology solutions provider.
2. The company is committed to creating maximum value for telecom operators.
3. In 2017, it achieved sales revenue of CNY 2 billion.
4. We have insisted on customer centricity.
5. Its vision is to enrich life through its products.

Situational conversations

Brief introduction

A: Nice to meet you. Could you please make a short introduction to your corporation?

B: With pleasure. Jiangsu Zhonghua High-tech Materials Co. Ltd. was founded in 1995.

Unit Six Enterprise Introduction

A: Where is the location of this corporation?
B: It locates in the Ocean Chemicals Zone of Suzhou.
A: What about its scale?
B: Its registered fund is 12 million US dollars and its plant occupies an area of 66,000 square meters.
A: How many workers does it employ?
B: About 260 employees work in the factory.
A: Oh, it's huge.

Corporate culture

A: How do you think of corporate culture?
B: It's necessary for every big company.
A: How about the culture of your company?
B: As a responsible chemical company, my company is constantly pursuing environmental protection policies.
A: What is the goal of your environmental protection policy?
B: In short, to seek to create a green chemical industry.
A: How do you realize this goal?
B: We are completely dedicated to technological innovation alongside sustainable growth and developing more eco-friendly, more advanced and more widespread bactericide industrial chains.
A: Could you make a summary of your culture policies?
B: Well, it's just to serve for a safer world, for better health and better life.

Product introduction

A: I want to know the main features of your product. Could you make an introduction?
B: No problem. This heating equipment is our featured product and it is equipped with digital lock.
A: Then what's the function of the digital lock?
B: It is used to realize auto-tracking.

A: It's great. What about other advantages?

B: It is light in weight, small in size and convenient in use. It is welcomed by its user-friendly design.

A: What about its application range?

B: It could be used for thermal treatment and induction heating.

After-sales service

A: Thank you very much for your prompt response to my call. I've found it a bit hard to get any good after-sales service these days.

B: I know what your mean. After-sales service is something our company takes very seriously.

A: It certainly makes a difference when I know the product is being properly supported.

B: I know a lot of companies tend to pay lip service and treat it as a nuisance.

A: That's exactly the impression I had with the electronics store where I bought my TV set.

B: What happened? Did you eventually get any satisfaction?

A: To start with, they wouldn't send out a serviceman and said I'd have to bring the set back to them.

B: How long had you kept the set before it played up?

A: It broke down less than a month after I bought it. It was under warranty and the salesmen said they would just replace it if there were any problems.

B: Salespeople do sometimes say things just to clinch the sale which may, or may not be, the company policy.

A: It certainly wasn't in this case because they took 2 weeks to repair and I had to go and pick it up.

B: Obviously, you don't have a very good impression of that company and, probably, will not recommend it to any of your friends.

A: Maybe it's true. But I cannot judge a company only by its after-sales service.

Unit Six Enterprise Introduction

Marketing

A: Good morning, Ms. Jane. How's your business?

B: Everything goes smoothly. I'm glad you come to our company again.

A: Thank you. Today, I'm going to do business with you and I'm interested in your garments.

B: Which kind of garments are you most interested in?

A: Skirt most. How is the supply position of this?

B: With regard to skirt, we can supply from stock.

A: Great, could you give me your price list?

B: Well, let me see, here you are.

A: The price list shows that the price of skirt is 11 US dollars per carton. I regret to say that your price is too high to accept. Could you give us a discount?

B: I'm afraid I couldn't grant your request. Considering you are a regular customer and we have been cooperating with pleasure for a long time, the lowest price we can offer you is 10.5 US dollars per carton, and you know, there's a little profit left for us.

A: OK, since this is your bottom price, I'll accept it, and I'd like to order 500 cartons. I wonder if it is possible for you to offer shipment before July.

B: Certainly, we can make it. We assure you that we will ship the goods in time.

Oral practice

I. **Talk with each other about the following questions or topics**

1. How to introduce this year's goal of your corporation?
2. How to make the next year's schedule about tech innovation for your company?
3. How to make a contribution to society which cultivates your corporation?
4. How to persuade new investors to put their money into your corporation?

II. **Situational practice**

1. The main purpose of a business is to maximize profits for its owners. Others contend that a business' principal purpose is to serve the interests of a larger

group of stakeholders, including employees, customers, and even society as a whole. Please talk about the different approaches your company employ in making profits.

2. A principal challenge for a business is to balance the interests of parties affected by the business, the interests that are sometimes in conflict with one another. An emerging new mantra is to create social progress as well as profits. If your customers want to know how you incorporate social responsibility with business profits, what would you like to say to them?

3. Business can also be viewed to exist for the purpose of creative expansion. Successful firms would manage to align their activities with the purpose of creative expansion. Suppose you are a software corporation manager, please talk about your innovation plan combining with the reality your corporation faces.

Complementary reading

Text A

Franchises

For many entrepreneurs and aspiring business owners, the prospect of starting a new business from scratch can be daunting, overwhelming, or even impossible due to financial restrictions on business loans. For these individuals, an alternative to forming a completely new business is the prospect of franchising, which allows an owner to "start" a new business venture while relying on the institutional knowledge and structure of an existing enterprise.

A franchise is the expansion of an existing trademark, service, or advertising approach to a new location through a business arrangement between the existing owner of the trademark or service and a new individual or group who would like to use that trademark or service to start a new business that expands upon the owner's existing set-up. A franchise agreement is created that sets forth the relationship between the franchisor (the existing owner) and the franchisee (the new business partner). Often, the franchisee will replicate the franchisor's business model in a new location, or will sell goods or services also offered by the franchisor. In so doing, the franchisee allows the franchisor to expand into a new market that he or she might not otherwise be able to reach, while the franchisor provides the franchisee with business advice and guidance that would be unavailable if the franchisee had simply started his or her own business from scratch.

Elements of a franchise

Franchises are governed by the United States Federal Trade Commission (FTC) and relevant state franchise laws. According to the FTC and its laws, a business relationship must have three components in order to be a franchise. First, the franchisee must have been given the right to provide goods or services under the trademark, service mark, trade name, logo, or other symbols of the franchisor. Second, the franchisor must retain significant control of or provide significant assistance for the franchisee's business. For instance, the franchisor may require the franchisee's business to look similar to the original business, to participate in the same promotional and sales campaigns as the original business, or to provide franchisor-approved training programs to all employees. Third, the franchisee must be required to pay a certain amount of money to the franchisor as a "fee" or "payment" for the trademark and services that the franchisor has provided.

Franchises are subject to strict regulation by the FTC and states, including regulation of the business relationship between the franchisor and the franchisee, disclosure requirements, and registration requirements. For this reason, it is very important for potential franchisees to carefully consider the FTC's rules and regulations, as well as the laws of their state, before formally agreeing to a franchising relationship.

Types of franchises

Franchises may vary depending on the degree of involvement of the franchisor in the business practices of the franchisee. One type of franchise relationship is known as product or trade name franchising. This occurs when the franchisee merely contracts with the franchisor to use the product, trademark, trade name, or commercial symbol of the original franchisor. A common example is a car dealership, where the franchisee sells the cars bearing the symbol of the franchisor. The second type of franchise relationship involves a more long-lasting business relationship, where the franchisee agrees to operate a business under a format virtually identical to that of the franchisor, known as "business format franchising". In this type of franchise, the franchisee imports not only the trademark and products of the franchisor, but also the business model. This is most commonly seen with businesses such as fast-food companies.

Weighing the pros and cons of a franchise

Determining whether to pursue a franchise as opposed to a new independent business is a difficult decision, and it often involves a close consideration of your own individual tolerance for risk or joint ownership. While a franchise offers significant opportunities for profit without the risk of starting a completely new business, it also often means relinquishing significant portions of control to an existing franchisor. Additionally, no matter the extent to which the profits of your business may be a result of your own hard work, they will likely be subject to a percentage taken by the franchisor as well as possible fees for training, equipment, and products.

> Text B

Partnerships

A partnership is a business owned by more than one person. There are several different types of partnerships, each with different characteristics, benefits, and possible disadvantages. A general partnership is the simplest form of a partnership. Generally, if a business is simply referred to as a "partnership", it is a general partnership.

General partnerships are easy to form

A business with two or more owners can be a partnership. Much like a sole proprietorship, forming a general partnership does not require filing any documents or taking any specific action. If you and another person simply run a business together, it is a general partnership by default. General partnerships differ in this regard from limited partnerships (LPs) or limited liability partnerships (LLPs), since forming one of those businesses requires documents to be filed with your state's Secretary of State or appropriate agency. Also, many states require general partners to register their business' name and pay taxes, even though the entity is technically formed without any formal process.

General partnerships give joint authority and impose joint liability

A general partnership can be thought of as an equal split between the partners. This offers benefits and possible disadvantages. Each partner has joint authority to act on behalf of the others, giving the entity a flexibility that other types of business structures do not have. Thus, one partner is free to contract with customers, suppliers, or other parties without the need for explicit approval from the other partners. However, since general partners share joint liability, contracts can be enforced against any of the partners. General partners may be held personally liable and are not offered the protections of a limited liability company (LLC) or LLP. It is therefore important to form a partnership only with people whom you trust.

Similarly, each general partner has an equal right to the profits and losses of the business. In the absence of an agreement that states otherwise, this is true no matter how much effort, capital, or other resources each partner puts into the business. If one partner chooses to leave the partnership, it is usually dissolved. The business must be re-formed between the remaining partners or run as some type of single-owner business if no partners remain.

For these reasons, it is a good idea for partners to create and agree to a partnership agreement. Even if it is not filed with the agency that regulates business in your state, a partnership agreement acts as a contract between the partners by outlining how profits are shared, how losses are accounted for, and how the business will be run. Having a solid partnership agreement in place may help avoid unnecessary conflicts between partners.

Taxes pass through to general partners' personal returns

The tax on a partnership passes through to the general partners, meaning they pay taxes for the business on their personal tax returns. In this way, general partnerships are similar to LLCs or S-corporations. A trade-off to this benefit is that

partners must usually pay the self-employment tax and quarterly estimated taxes. Be sure to consult a tax professional if you are unsure about the taxes you may owe due to your general partnership or other business.

Tasks

■ Task 1 Vocabulary development

Read the following words and expressions. Try to keep them in mind and find more to enrich your language bank.

A. Useful words and expressions

BD (business development)	业务拓展
FMCC (fast moving consumer goods)	快速消费品
feedback	反馈
financial controller	财务总监或财政监督官
financial officer	财务主管
GM (general manager)	总经理
HR (human resource)	人力资源
headcount	人员编制
merchandising manager	采购经理
marketing director	市场总监
offer	聘书
PM (project manager)	项目经理
qualify	资质
quota	指标
reference	资料
senior accountant-AP	高级会计—应付
team building	团队建设
team leader	团队负责人
transportation & logistics	物流与仓储
value	利益

B. Sample sentences

Company details	· ABC Co., Ltd., established in 2017, is a high-tech company involved in R&D, production and selling of mobile phones and relative electronic materials. · CBA Co., Ltd., established in 2016, is a unique enterprise in LCD production. · Hebei Machinery Equipment Co., Ltd. is a mining machinery company mainly engaged in manufacturing ... · Our factory covers over 45,000 square meters, has now over 500 employees, more than 20 middle and senior technicians, over 20,000 square meters of high standard plant building and modern offices, R&D center and sales center. · We have developed substantial competencies in the areas of high-quality fine chemicals includes ... · The products are widely applied to the fields of personal care & cosmetics, household & institutional cleansers, health care industry, food, pesticide, agriculture, fragrances & flavors, etc.
Company qualifications	· We focus on the construction and implement ation of modern enterprise management system and operate in accordance with ISO 201314516 quality system since establishment. · Our products have acquired ISO1348523 Certificates, AFDA Certificates and CE Certificates ... · Based on strong technology, complete scientific management system and high quality of products, ABC Co., Ltd. has quickly grown into an important production and export base of China. Our products have been exported to over 80 countries, widely used in global mining and the construction industry.
Company culture	· We are working on creating a comfortable medical environment for the patients around the world. · To make safety and happiness with science and technology. · Sincerity. Profession. Innovation. Win-Win. · Customers first. Honest and credible. Mutual benefit. · We understand that our customers' needs, and our mission and values. So the develop ment strategy, price, operation mode and any business decisions we made are all to meet our customers' needs. · Serve for a safer world—Better Health, Better Life.

	· As a responsible chemical company, ABC is constantly pursuing environmental protection policies, and seeking to create a green chemical industry.
Services provided	· We provide customers all over the world with the best efficiency, highest security and best service. · We provide advanced video security monitoring solution and cloud service. · Taizhou Bytops Systems Co., Ltd. is a leading integrated video communication system solution provider, and incorporates research and development, design, production and sales. · Sincere, enthusiastic sales and a customer-service team, a professional, integrity, experienced technical team, promote each other, mutual cooperation, and provide customers with products and services of the best quality.

■ Task 2   Cultural salon

Read the following passage and try to get some knowledge about corporations.

Corporations in the US

In a general sense, a corporation is a business entity that is given many of the same legal rights as an actual person. Corporations may be made up of a single person or a group of people, known as sole corporations or aggregate corporations respectively.

Corporations exist as virtual or fictitious persons, granting a limited protection to the actual people involved in the business of the corporation. This limitation of liability is one of the many advantages to incorporation, and is a major draw for smaller businesses to incorporate; particularly those involved in highly litigated trade.

A company is incorporated in a specific nation, often within the bounds of a smaller subset of that nation, such as a state or province. The corporation is then governed by the laws of incorporation in that state.

A corporation may issue stocks, either private or public, or may be classified as a non-stock corporation. If stocks are issued, the corporation will usually be governed by its shareholders, either directly or indirectly. The most common model is a board of directors who make all major decisions for the corporation, in theory serving the best interests of the individual shareholders.

In the United States there are three major types of corporations: Close, C, and S.

Close corporations issue stocks, but the amount of shareholders is greatly limited, usually to less than thirty. Given the small number of shareholders, normally all are involved in board-level decision-making. The transfer and sale of stocks are also tightly controlled.

C corporations are the most common type of corporations in the United States. They allow theoretically unlimited amounts of stocks to be issued, and usually have a smaller board of directors who make decisions. C corporations pay taxes both at the corporate level and at the personal level, as shareholders pay taxes on their dividends.

S corporations are virtually identical to C corporations, save that they have a special tax status with the Internal Revenue Service (IRS). Instead of paying taxes at both levels, S corporations are required only to tax their dividends—the corporation itself does not need to pay taxes.

While many people in the United States choose to incorporate in their own state, small businesses especially, some states have corporate charters that are particularly beneficial to certain types of business. Nevada, for example, does not require ownership records that attach names, making it ideal for corporations interested in protecting the private identities of their owners.

A number of books and websites have sprung up in recent years to aid small businesses to incorporate. There are two major benefits for most small businesses. The first is the substantial legal and fiscal protection in the event of litigation or bankruptcy. The second is a potentially uninterrupted, essentially infinite lifespan for the business. This is contrasted with a sole proprietorship, which may experience problems and complications should the owner die, while a corporation allows the seamless passing on of the business.

Different states have different fees for incorporation, but most are extremely affordable. For anything more complicated than a simple sole proprietorship incorporation, an attorney is a necessity; and even for the most basic corporate structure, legal counsel is recommended.

Unit Seven Marketing & Promotion

Unit Seven

Marketing & Promotion

 Unit objectives

After learning this unit, you should
- find ways to improve your oral skills and performance;
- master basic words and expressions about marketing and promotion;
- know some cultural background knowledge about marketing and promotion.

Preparing

I. Useful words and expressions

1. 试销
2. 畅销货
3. 销路
4. 销售代理商
5. 促销
6. 市场分割,市场细分
7. 潜在顾客
8. 营销组合
9. 销售费用
10. 卖方市场
11. current customer
12. selling profit
13. selling technique
14. marketing strategy
15. consumer promotion
16. sales forecast
17. shelf display
18. promotional activity
19. competitor information
20. sales target

II. Useful sentences

1. Your bicycles can find a ready market in the eastern part of our country.

2. We are sure that you can sell more this year according to the marketing conditions at your end.

3. According to your estimate, what is the maximum annual turnover you could fulfill?

4. We've spared no effort in promoting the sales of your products.

5. We've learnt that you have years of experience in pushing the sales of porcelain products.

Situational conversations

Market research

A: Did you get a good response from a discounted introductory price?

B: We've just carried out a survey of both consumers and retailers regarding our future sound cards.

A: Did you get a good response from the telephone survey? A lot of people won't give market researchers the time of day on the telephone.
B: That may be true at home. But we called people at office numbers and found some people were more willing to talk on company time.
A: Really? What did they say?
B: Well, it looks like our plans for a fully functional but low end sound card were right on.
A: People are looking for cheaper ones?
B: Of course. Price is an important variable in our market, so we can use it to build our customer base.
A: Right. They want low prices, but most important of all, the cards must be reliable.

Advertising

A: We want to use the right marketing mix to reach our target market.
B: Certainly. We've done some tactical planning already. We think we've come up with a good plan.
A: What kinds of media do you plan to use?
B: Well, taking into account the image you want to project, we've asked our copywriters to prepare copies for computer magazines and the Internet first.
A: So that way, our advertising dollars would be focused on people we know that are computer users.
B: Yes. We'll also run billboard and newspaper ads to help create broad brand recognition.
A: Will there be any direct mail?
B: No. That would not be correct for a manufacturer like you. Leave that to the retailers.
A: Good point. Please prepare a more detailed proposal, and then I'll pitch it to the higher-ups.
B: Great. We'll get started right away.

Promotional activities

A: As you know, the Fast Trek 4000 is due for release next month. I think we've finally worked the kinks out.

B: Great. That's vital. Quality is the focus of the ad campaign. The boards must work well if they're going to be the cash cow we want them to be.

A: Let's go over our promotion plans again.

B: OK. We have six major retailers running demonstrations at most branches. And our exhibition team is already on the road setting up for computer shows.

A: Good. What about print and radio?

B: We've taken out full-page ads for two large trade magazines. And more important, our press releases have been well received.

A: Any larger ads?

B: Yes. We're putting the same full-page ad in the Sunday edition of three major newspapers.

A: Sounds perfect.

B: But nothing ever works out as you want it. So I have a number of other tricks up my sleeve as well.

Promotion

A: I understand your company is in need of new computer equipment?

B: Yes, we're doing an overhaul of the office and all its equipment.

A: Well, I might be able to help you there; the company I represent is a major provider of a wide range of quality computer equipment.

B: Oh yeah? There are 500 other computer companies out there. What makes your products so special?

A: Because not only do we custom build the equipment to your requirements but our computers and after-sales service are first-class.

B: Really? You can custom build to our needs?

A: Certainly. We have our own computer specialists and engineers that can not only build your required systems, but also install all the necessary software and

networks.
B: That sounds great. I haven't heard that offered before.
A: I assure you, ma'am. You won't find better. Can I give you a few brochures that will further explain what we can offer?
B: Sure.

Product introduction

A: This is the model I was interested in.
B: I should be very happy to give you any further information you need on it.
A: Yes. What are the specifications?
B: If I may refer you to the brochure you'll find all the specifications there.
A: Ah, yes. Now what about the service life?
B: Our tests indicate that this model has a service life of at least four years.
A: Is that an average figure for this type of equipment?
B: Oh no, far from it. That's about one year longer than any other make in its price range.
A: Now what happens if something goes wrong when we're using it?
B: If that were to happen, please contact our nearest agent and he'll send someone round immediately.

Product quality

A: I can promise you that, if you buy our product, you will be getting quality.
B: I've looked at your units, and I am very happy with them. Your goods are all far above standard quality.
A: We spend a lot of money to make sure that our quality is much better. We don't sacrifice quality for quick profits.
B: Well, we're really interested in placing an order under negotiation. We can start the negotiation as soon as you want.
A: That's great. I'm glad we'll be able to do business together. I'll have some quotes ready for you by tomorrow morning.
B: Fine. Also, would you mind if I ask to see a surveyor's report of your

products? I may have a few more questions about your quality analysis.

Oral practice

I. Talk with each other about the following questions or topics

1. What is important to you when you buy a product like a computer or a TV?

2. What are the ways in which your body will tell the other person that you are listening attentively?

3. What do you think are the important and good qualities of a salesperson? Among them, which is the most important one?

4. Communication is very important in the process of product promotion. Then, how to make communication more effective?

II. Situational practice

1. Suppose you are Tanya Nichols, the owner of an ice cream manufacturing company. You are talking with the marketing manager, Carla Hudson, about the advertising campaign for the company's new ice cream sandwich.

2. You are a salesperson of Sea Gull Soap Powder. Mr. Robert Anderson is quite interested in your new formula G2 soap powder. He wants to know more details about the product, including specifications, new features, and after-sales service, etc.

3. Suppose you are a salesperson of Sunivision Security Camera Company. You are calling Mr. James Ma, hoping to market your new product—Smart Home WiFi wireless IP Camera. You also try to arrange a meeting with him so as to show how your product works.

Unit Seven Marketing & Promotion

Complementary reading

Text A

Ladies and Gentlemen,

May I have your attention, please? Thanks for attending the negotiation conference. Today I'm going to show you our new product. It's an electronic clock. I'm certain you will find its advantages after my introduction. Now let's take a look at it.

It was made from aluminum alloy, a kind of hard material, which can prevent the stuff you want to hold from being stolen. The distinction of our product is its very high quality and compact size. With people's increasing feelings of insecurity, it's necessary to make us feel protected. The phenomenon is global. I'm pretty sure that our product will be competitive in the international market. Our company has been developing this kind of products for several years, and its price is feasible. It has been on the market for a short time in China, and the profits it had brought is satisfactory.

I hope this product will bring more benefits to you and we can have a win-win cooperation. Thank you.

Text B

A: Okay, here are the graphs and figures for this month's sales. Let's review them all together.

B: The first one, I have a question ... This graph is marking the sales performance for our line of hair products, right? Can this line be right? It looks like our sales plummeted. I can't believe we did that poorly ... If I remember correctly, sales went down slightly, but not as dramatically as the graph shows.

A: I think you are looking at the wrong line. The rapid drop in sales wasn't our hair products. You are correct. The sales of the hair product decreased slightly, but not dramatically. The one that didn't do so hot this month was the cleaning

products. I think there was a problem in the marketing plan. Some people were offended by our advertisements for the cleaning products, but it was already too late to mitigate the damage, so our mistake shows up in the sales.

B: Well, the good news is the new industrial cleaning products really took off. Look how the sales have shot up over the last two weeks.

A: That is our one major success. If you look at the other graphs, you can see that most of the other product lines remain steady with little increase.

B: At least they stay the same. That's better than dropping.

Tasks

Task 1 Vocabulary development

Read the following words and expressions. Try to keep them in mind and find more to enrich your language bank.

A. Useful words and expressions

品牌兴趣	brand interest
品牌忠诚	brand loyalty
品牌定位	brand positioning
品牌识别	brand recognition
品牌战略	brand strategy
品牌扩展	brand extension
消费行为	consumer behavior
需求层次	hierarchy of needs
人际影响	interpersonal influence
参照人群	reference group
地理人口细分	geodemographic segmentation
消费心态细分	psychographic segmentation
引入期	introductory phase
成长期	growth stage
成熟期	maturity stage

Unit Seven Marketing & Promotion

特许品牌	licensed brand
全国性品牌	national brand
产品生命周期	product life cycle
宣传	publicity
垂直营销体系	vertical marketing system
网络营销	network/Internet marketing
广告软文	advertorial
情感诉求	emotional appeal
理性诉求	rational appeal
消费者洞察	consumer insight
点击成本	cost per click (CPC)
千人成本	cost per thousand impressions (CPM)
创意黄金塔	creative pyramid
数字营销	digital marketing
电子优惠券	e-coupon
整合营销	integrated marketing
互动营销/广告	interactive marketing/advertising
线上营销	online marketing
搜索引擎营销	search engine marketing (SEM)
流媒体	streaming

B. Sample sentences

Product recommendation	· Enclosed is our new product catalogue for your reference. If there is any enquiry, please feel free to contact us. · We are proud to let you know that our DF610 trendy wireless headphone has received lots of positive feedback from our customers. · I guess you are busy preparing for new products of the new year. Currently, BT headsets are considered as a necessity in people's business life. More and more businessmen use wireless headsets to talk when on the road or driving a car.

	· Our factory has launched a new CSR 4.1 Sporty headset; I guess it will probably meet your demand. · This is our most recently developed products. · Its durability will be an agreeable surprise to you. · With its incredibly small size and feather light weight, XXX is perfect for listening to music or answering phone calls on the move.
Product introduction	· This kind of bicycle can be folded in half and handy to carry around, especially useful during traveling and traffic jams. · The handbags we quoted are all made of the best leather and have various kinds and styles in order to meet the requirements of all walks of life in your country. · Owning to its superior quality and reasonable price our silk has met with warm reception and quick sale in most European countries.
Product quality	· By virtue of its super quality, this product is often sold out in many areas. · Our quality is based solely on our sales samples. · We sell goods as per the sales sample, not the quality of any previous supplies. · You can see the difference between these grades. · No doubt you've received the samples of the inferior quality. · If the quality of your products is satisfactory, we may place regular orders.
Promotion	· We have some special offers. · How many pieces would you like to order? · May I know what items you are interested in? · Where would you like us to deliver the goods? · If this color is not available, would you like another one? · We will try our best to deliver it ASAP. · Hope you will be our business partner!
Prices	· Are these prices wholesale or retail? · They start at 150 *yuan* and go up to 200 *yuan*. · The price is unreasonable. · Taking the quality into consideration, I think the price is reasonable. · It's not possible for us to make any sales at this price. · Your price is higher than that of other companies. · Can you make it a little cheaper? /Can you come down a little? /Can you reduce the price?

Task 2 Cultural salon

Read the following passage and try to get some knowledge about Internet marketing.

Opportunities in online international marketing

International marketing is no longer an option, but a strategic imperative. Businesses that focus primarily on their domestic markets will be left behind as their competitors gain "first mover advantage" in the international marketplace. When we consider that the Unites States only represents 4 percent of the world's population, opportunities to sell our products and services worldwide become clearly evident.

The growth of the Internet has increased competition tremendously and opened up the doors to international business. Companies have developed a web presence to keep themselves ahead or in line with their competitors internationally. In addition to gaining a competitive advantage, there are a number of additional reasons why a company's web presence is becoming an increasingly important tool to reach global markets.

Internet population—Internet access is increasing in regions throughout the world. According to Computer Industry Almanac, 533 million people have access to the Internet, which represents approximately 8 percent of the world's population. Aberdeen Group predicts that by the end of 2005, 17 percent of worldwide population will have Internet access.

E-commerce growth—According to International Data Corporation (IDC), the US accounts for approximately 40 percent of all money spent online, but that percentage is expected to decrease as Western Europe and Asia increase their online spending. According to Aberdeen Group, by 2003, 66 percent of E-commerce spending will originate outside the United States.

Demand for products and services—Regions throughout the world are realizing the enormous information resource the Web is and are interested in content, and products and services that their own regions do not provide.

Online payment—A barrier that blocked E-commerce growth throughout the world, particularly in Europe, was different currencies. However, adoption of the Euro is completed, phasing out local currencies and blurring borders between countries in the European Union. By enabling better price comparisons, increasing competition and improving deals for online buyers, the Euro is making it easier to conduct business in the European online market and providing better entry for non-European companies.

Marketing and advertising—Online marketing is a popular method to gain international audiences. For example, email has become one of the most successful channels for marketers in Europe, which means that companies interested in selling to the European online market should take advantage of this popular medium.

Increased sales and reduced costs—A website provides an avenue through which to gain access to a large audience without spending a lot of money. For example, it cuts down on paper costs associated with direct marketing and magazine or newspaper advertising.

Unit Eight　Business Negotiation

Unit Eight

Business Negotiation

 Unit objectives

After learning this unit, you should
- find out the basic procedures in business negotiation;
- master the basic words and expressions about business negotiation;
- know some cultural background knowledge about business negotiation.

Preparing

I. Useful words and expressions

1. 不可撤销信用证
2. 让步
3. 汇款协议
4. 延期付款
5. 通融
6. 供贵方参考
7. 汇付
8. 即期付款交单
9. 承兑交单
10. 到岸价/船上交货价
11. shipping mark
12. the stipulated terms
13. be tied up
14. prevailing economic crisis
15. usual practice
16. in our favor
17. negotiation in China
18. bill of exchange
19. execute the order
20. issue an invoice

II. Useful sentences

1. I believe you're going out of your way for us.
2. Wouldn't you like to spend an extra day or two here?
3. I'm afraid that won't be possible, much as we'd like to.
4. I wonder if it is possible to arrange shopping for us.
5. I will keep you posted.

Situational conversations

Specific inquiry

A: Well, we are thinking of placing an order. We are interested in the electronic products of your company. We hope to have your lowest offer, CIF Liverpool.

B: Thank you for your inquiry. Could you please let us know the quantity you require?

A: Here is a list of our requirements.

B: Here are our FOB price lists. All prices in the lists are subject to our final

confirmation. You will find the prices are reasonable.
A: Could we meet again tomorrow afternoon for further details?
B: Sure.

Firm offer and counter-offer

A: Nice to meet you again, Mr. Smith.
B: Glad to meet you, too. We have the offer ready for you. Here it is. 1,000 sets of CD players at US $150 each, CIF Liverpool, for shipment in January. The offer is valid for five days.
A: Your price is almost 20% higher than last year's.
B: Mr. Smith, you know the demand for the CD players has soared a great deal recently.
A: I must point out that your price is higher than some of the quotations we have received from other companies.
B: But you must take the quality into account.
A: I admit that your products may be of better quality. But it would be hard for us to get the products promoted without the moderate prices. What about US $120 each set?
B: It is too low for us and leaves no profit margin.
A: Let me explain for you why we think the price is reasonable. The competition is quite fierce in the small appliance area. It is shown that the reasonable price of the CD player is around 90 – 120 each set.
B: Well, I think both of us need to make a concession.

Acceptance

A: Good morning, Mr. Smith.
B: Good morning, Mr. Black.
A: We have considered your counter-offer yesterday, but it is a little bit too much for us. But we are ready to reduce our price from US $150 to US $140 each set if your quantity is not less than 2,000 sets considering our long friendly business relationship.

B: We accept the quantity, but for this quantity, our final counter-offer requires US $130 each set. We hope you will consider it again.

A: All right. That is a deal.

Placing an order and confirmation

A: We made a concession at last!

B: Thank you for your concession and we are satisfied with the price.

A: So you could place your orders now. The offer is valid only for three days.

B: We will order 2,000 sets of CD players at US $130 each, CIF Liverpool, for shipment in January.

A: We can confirm your orders: 2,000 CD players and the unit price is US $130 each, CIF Liverpool, shipment in January.

B: All right. Hope you make the delivery on time.

Terms of payment

A: Well, we have settled almost everything about the deal, except the terms of payment.

B: For payment of this order, we would like to make the payment by D/P or D/A, for this has not been our initial deal.

A: To be frank, it is impossible for us to accept D/A and D/P because of the considerable risk we'll take. We can only accept payment by confirmed irrevocable L/C payable against shipment documents.

B: Can we make the payment by L/C after sight? When we apply for an L/C, we have to pay a sum of deposit, which will surely increase our cost. Could you make accommodation this time?

A: Taking your high reputation into consideration, we agree to accept payment by L/C 30 days after sight.

Oral practice

I. Talk with each other about the following questions or topics

1. What are the basic principles of business negotiation?

2. What do you think of the influences of psychology and culture on business negotiation?

3. If you are asked to make a negotiating plan for a coming negotiation, on what should you base your plan? What main issues should be included in your plan?

4. What are the roles of a CN (chief negotiator)? Can you add any other qualities about a CN?

II. Situational practice

1. Suppose you are the supplier of a company, you try to make a quotation directly to your regular customers and to others who may be interested in your products without waiting for inquiries. How should you begin your conversation?

2. If you would like to make a firm offer to your customers, what are the contents you should include?

3. As is known to us all, negotiation on price is one of the most important factors in international business activities, which we should treat with great caution. So when the price negotiation is undergoing, what are the factors we should show our concern to when dealing with pricing?

Complementary reading

Text A

A: Mr. Smith, as to your inquiry for 500 metric tons of corn, we've worked it out and that's $100 per MT FOB and the price is valid for five days.

B: Why? Your price has increased so greatly. It's almost 25% higher than last year's. It's really hard for us to accept it.

A: I'm so surprised to hear that. Mr. Smith, as you know the price for corn has increased sharply in recent years. Our price is rather lower than the prices prevailing in the world market. And the quality of our products is better than others.

B: Of course, your products may be of higher quality, but considering the target clients in our country, the moderate prices would be more appropriate.

A: We fixed our price at this level based on sophisticated survey, so you do not need to worry about the promotion.

B: To finalize our business, I am afraid that you have to reduce your price by at least 20%.

A: You mean 20%? That's quite impossible.

B: How about 15% then? This is the highest price we can accept. Anything higher than this, we'll give up the deal.

A: I am afraid we can't, for this is the best we can offer.

Text B

A: I checked the catalog you gave me this morning, and I'd like to discuss prices on your catalog.

B: All right. Here is our price list.

A: I see that your listed price for the portable computer LN999 is $500. Do you offer quantity discounts?

B: Sure. We give a 10% discount for orders of 100 or more.

A: What kind of discount could you give me if I were to place an order of 500 units?

B: In that case, we can give you a 15% discount.

A: What about the delivery time?

B: We could ship your order within 30 days of receiving your payment.

A: Do you require payment in advance of shipment?

B: You may open a letter of credit in our favor.

A: OK, that's the deal. I'd like to go ahead and place an order for 500 units.

B: Marvelous! Let's sign the contract now.

Unit Eight Business Negotiation

Tasks

■ Task 1 Vocabulary development

Read the following words and expressions. Try to keep them in mind and find more to enrich your language bank.

A. Useful words and expressions

随函寄去,请查收……	enclosed please find …
宣传资料	literature
会计报表	accounting statement
采购单	purchase list
订货通知单	order slip
及时回复	reply in due course
商业礼仪	business protocol
首次亮相	debut
激烈的竞争	keen competition
价格正在上涨	the price is on the rise
达成交易	strike the bargain
补贴	subsidy
速遣费	dispatch money
保修期	warranty period
国际结算	international settlement
托收	collection
信用证	letter of credit(L/C)
银行保函	letter of guarantee(L/G)
商业发票	commercial invoice/paper
装箱单	packing list
产地证	certificate of origin
保险单	insurance policy
海运提单	marine bill of lading(B/L)

国际惯例	international practice
预付货款/随订单付款	cash on order
交单付款	cash against order
交货付现	cash on delivery
订货时付款	cash with order
现金订货	make cash order
达成和解,达成妥协	come to an accommodation
重申	reiterate
资金/资信状况	financial status
信用交易,赊欠交易	deal on credit

B. Sample sentences

Opening speech	• To begin with, I'd like to make a brief introduction of the current market. • Before I begin, let's make it clear that it's only a non-formal talk. • We are pleased to receive your inquiry, for which we thank you very much. • Thank you for your inquiry, in which you enquired about the details of our products. • Firstly, let me outline the current problems we are facing. • Let's see if our solution is workable. • Now, we'll go into details of these accidents. • Today, we will discuss how to execute our contract smoothly.
Transfer the topic	• Now let's move on to the next issue. • I'm glad that we have reached an agreement on the issue. There remains only the question of shipment. • What shall we discuss next? I suggest we have a word about insurance.
Reiterate	• You said just now that competition could be quite fierce. But I think I have made it clear that D/A is absolutely impossible. • Earlier, you mentioned that this kind of product was in great demand. • As I said just now, any money spent now would give you greater savings in the long run. • Weren't you suggesting that we put these words down in the contract as a special clause?

Stress	· Let me emphasize how necessary it is to abide by the contract. · I can't stress enough the disastrous consequences of breach of contract. · I must call your attention to the distinction between these two samples. · I must stress that goods were strictly inspected before shipment.
Repeat	· Would you mind saying it again? /Will you repeat it, please? /I beg your pardon? · I'm sorry I didn't catch your meaning. Will you say it again? · I don't understand what you say. /I'm sorry I don't follow you. · Would you explain what you mean? /Could you be more specific?
Disagreement	· It's absolutely impossible. I really can't accept the idea. · I don't like the idea of substituting the goods we ordered. · I'm sorry. I disagree with you there.
Ask for opinion	· What do you think of it? /How would you like it to be? · What's your opinion on this matter? We'd like you to give us your suggestions. · How do you see things like this? · Will you let me know your comments on our new design? · Your comments and criticisms are always welcome.

■ Task 2 Cultural salon

Read the following passage and try to get some knowledge about business negotiation.

Face-to-face negotiation

About the opening speech

It's hard to break the ice. When an opening speech is needed you could have the following alternatives. You could use a completely irrelevant topic to start off the meeting. You could talk about the weather, or you could show to others your interests in the city and even focus on the hobbies. Sometimes you could also apply a humorous story to lighten the tension to achieve bettering communication and try to generate a friendly and harmonious atmosphere and avoid a defending psychology.

Two typical tactics on bid

When dealing with the bid, you could either prefer the Western-European style or the Asian-Japanese way. The first emphasizes on proposing virtual head price with wider defensible scale. And in that case you could compare the strength of buyers and sellers and lubricate and approach the buyer's market and the conditions; The latter, you should always utilize the lowest prices listed on the bid sheet to attract the buyers. And the payment must be the most favorable to the sellers.

Guidelines for answering the questions in the negotiation

Do not answer initiatively more than what is being asked. It means the seller should not respond initiatively. Just answer what you are asked to avoid the consequences of "loose lips sink ships". Answer clearly what is being asked. It refers to that all the relevant issues raised by the other party must be answered one by one very smoothly and straightforwardly.

Unit Nine Business Meeting

Unit Nine

Business Meeting

 Unit objectives

After learning this unit, you should
- find ways to improve your oral skills and performance;
- master basic words and expressions about business meetings;
- know some cultural background knowledge about business meetings.

Preparing

Ⅰ. Useful words and expressions

1. 休会
2. 会议议程
3. 赞成
4. 反对
5. 弃权
6. 假如你问我,我认为
7. 太对了
8. 我明白你的意思
9. 欢迎会
10. regular meeting
11. pending
12. reach a consensus
13. high-level talk
14. settle all disputes amicably by negotiation
15. put/place sth. on the agenda
16. the minutes
17. minute-taker
18. clarify one's position

Ⅱ. Useful sentences

1. Can/May I have your attention, please?
2. The agenda of the meeting is as follows.
3. Could you be a little more specific?
4. Let's summarize what we've said so far.
5. It looks as if we've covered the main items. The meeting is closed.

Situational conversations

Introduction

(*A = Meeting Chairman, B = Jack Peterson, C = Margaret Simmons*)

A: If we are all here, let's get started. First of all, I'd like you to join me in welcoming Jack Peterson, our Southwest Area Sales Vice President.

B: Thank you for having me! I'm looking forward to today's meeting.

A: I'd also like to introduce Margaret Simmons who recently joined our team.

C: May I also introduce my assistant, Bob Hamp?

Unit Nine Business Meeting

A: Welcome Bob. I'm afraid our national sales director, Anne Trusting, can't be with us today. She is in Kobe at the moment, developing our Far East sales force.

Reviewing past business

(A = Meeting Chairman, B = Tom Johnson)

A: Let's get started. We're here today to discuss ways of improving sales in rural market areas. First, let's go over the report from the last meeting which was held on June 24th. All right, Tom, over to you.

B: Thank you, Mark. Let me just summarize the main points of the last meeting. We began the meeting by approving the changes in our sales reporting system discussed on May 30th. After briefly revising the changes that would take place, we moved on to a brainstorming session concerning after-sales customer support improvements. You'll find a copy of the main ideas developed and discussed in these sessions in the photocopies in front of you. The meeting was declared closed at 11:30 a.m.

Discussing items

(A = Meeting Chairman, B = Jack Peterson, C = Donald Smith,
D = Alice Jones, E = Bob Hamp, F = Jennifer Brown)

A: Thank you, Tom. So, if there is nothing else we need to discuss, let's move on to today's agenda. Have you all received a copy of today's agenda? If you don't mind, I'd like to skip Item 1 and move on to Item 2: Sales improvement in rural market areas. Jack has kindly agreed to give us a report on this matter. Jack?

B: Before I begin the report, I'd like to get some ideas from you all. How do you feel about rural sales in your sales districts? I suggest we go round the table first to get all of your input.

C: In my opinion, we have been focusing too much on urban customers and their needs. The way I see things, we need to return to our rural base by developing an advertising campaign to focus on their particular needs.

D: I'm afraid I can't agree with you. I think rural customers want to feel as important as our customers living in cities. I suggest we give our rural sales teams more help with advanced customer information reporting.

E: Excuse me, I didn't catch that. Could you repeat that, please?

D: I just stated that we need to give our rural sales teams better customer information reporting.

C: I don't quite follow you. What exactly do you mean?

D: Well, we provide our city sales staff with database information on all of our larger clients. We should provide the same sort of knowledge on our rural customers to our sales staff there.

B: Would you like to add anything, Jennifer?

F: I must admit I never thought about rural sales that way before. I have to agree with Alice.

B: Well, let me begin with this PowerPoint presentation. As you can see, we are developing new methods to reach out to our rural customers.

C: I suggest we break up into groups and discuss the ideas we've seen presented.

Finishing the meeting

(A = Meeting Chairman, B = Jack Peterson, C = Donald Smith)

A: Unfortunately, we're running short of time. We'll have to leave that to another time.

B: Before we close, let me just summarize the main points: Rural customers need special help to feel more valued. Our sales teams need more accurate information on our customers. A survey will be completed to collect data on spending habits in these areas. The results of this survey will be delivered to our sales teams. We are considering specific data mining procedures to help deepen our understanding.

A: Thank you very much, Jack. Right, it looks as though we've covered the main items. Is there any other business?

C: Can we fix the next meeting, please?

A: Good idea, Donald. How does Friday in two weeks' time sound to everyone?

Let's meet at the same time, 9 o'clock. Is that OK for everyone? Excellent. I'd like to thank Jack for coming to our meeting today. The meeting is closed.

Oral practice

I. Talk with each other about the following questions or topics

1. What is a meeting agenda?
2. Why do we need to write a meeting agenda?
3. What is the purpose of minutes?
4. Who writes the minutes?
5. What do the minutes contain?
6. How can you become a successful chairman of a meeting?
7. Describe a memorable meeting you have ever chaired.

II. Situational practice

1. Suppose you are having a meeting to discuss about the best candidate to be the monitor of your class. Choose one of you as the chairman, another as the note-taker, and yet another as the representative who will report your meeting to the class.

2. Discuss with your partner about the general procedures of holding a meeting and the necessary preparations for each step.

3. Suppose here is a meeting on progress. Chairman—presides the meeting. Speaker A—says that the television campaign has proved an enormous success and proposed an increase in export. Speaker B—asks the chairman if it would be possible to arrange a farewell dinner for the Sales Manager who has been with the company for 25 years and now is due to retire early because of ill health; asks if the chairman could be prepared to make a speech at the dinner.

Complementary reading

Text A

An American company sent a representative to negotiate a contract with a Japanese firm. The American representative arrived at the appointed time for this meeting and was shown to the meeting room where six representatives from the Japanese firm were waiting for him. When the representative was doing his presentation, the Japanese moved their heads in an up and down motion. They said very little. The presentation was given in English as the representative had been told the Japanese understood English. When the representative asked if there were any questions, everybody nodded politely; however, no one said a word. After a few minutes, the representative asked if they were ready to sign the contract. One of the Japanese said, "It is very difficult for us to sign." At that point the representative said, "Should I leave the contract with you?" The Japanese said, "Yes." The representative returned to America expecting the Japanese to return the contract, which did not happen.

This case tells us that in order to avoid being frustrated, an individual should be full aware of cultural conflicts in a cross-cultural working environment.

Text B

(A = Ms. Nicholson, B = Mr. Wong)

A (*in the main office*): Mr. Wong, where is your project report? You said you'd get it done soon. I need your part of the report so that I can finish my final report by the end of this week. When do you think you can get it done?

B (*hesitantly*): Well ... Ms. Nicholson ... I didn't realize the deadline was so soon ... I will try my best to get it done as soon as possible. It's just that there are lots of details I need to crosscheck ... I'm really not sure ...

A (*frustrated*): Mr. Wong, how soon is soon? I really need to know your plan of action right now. You cannot be so vague in answering my questions all

Unit Nine Business Meeting

that time. I believe I've given you plenty of time to work on this report already.

B (*a long pause*): Well ... I'm really not sure, Ms. Nicholson, I really don't want to do a bad job on the report and disappoint you; I'll try my best to finish it as soon as possible. Maybe I can finish the report next week.

Tasks

Task 1 Vocabulary development

Read the following words and expressions. Try to keep them in mind and find more to enrich your language bank.

A. Useful words and expressions

缺席	absence
议题	agenda item
分配,配给	allocate
分配任务	allocate task
随时	at short notice
出席者	attendance
听众席,会堂	auditorium
董事会会议室	board room
头脑风暴	brainstorming
流通,发行	circulate
阐明,介绍	clarify
合作的	collaborative
会议	conference
一致同意	consensus
代表	delegate
离题	digress
引出,推导出	elicit
提供信息的	informative
询问,调查	inquire into

主要发言人	keynote speaker
提议,动议	motion
临时日程	provisional agenda
审定日程	approved agenda
议项,项目	proceedings
准时的	punctual
提出	put forward
饮料,小食	refreshments
剩下的时间不多了	run out of time
超过规定时间	run over time
座位安排	seating arrangement
专题讨论会	seminar
举手表决	show of hands
大声发言	speak up
讨论会,座谈会	symposium
投票表决	take a vote
离题	digress from the point
一致同意的	unanimous
会议地点	venue
电视会议	videoconference
详细记述	write up

B. Sample sentences

| Opening a meeting | · Can/May I have your attention, please?
· Ladies and gentlemen, I need your attention.
· Shall we begin? /Let's get started.
· I declare the meeting open.
· I'm glad to see that you could all make it to this meeting.
· As you can see from the agenda, we have 3 points for discussion.
· We're meeting today to discuss … Well, let me begin with this PowerPoint presentation.
· This should take about three hours.
· The meeting is due to finish at 12:00 o'clock.
· I'd like to keep each item to thirty minutes. |

Controlling a meeting	· I don't think it's related to our topic. · Grace, please do not digress from the topic. · Mike, you're digressing from the subject. · We will come to that point later. · Shall we move on to the next item on the agenda? · It seems as though we've covered that main points. · In conclusion/In short/In a word, we've discussed three points. · To sum up, there seem to be four plans we can choose from. · So, Ann, you're going to write up a proposal. · It seems we've discussed everything, so let's close the meeting.
Participating in a meeting	· I'd like to draw your attention to this chart/table. · I have prepared a PowerPoint to illustrate this. · How do you feel about this proposal? · What's your view on this? · Would you like to comment, Nora? · Why don't you speak first, Tom? · Is there anyone who'd like to say something? · Mr. Chairman, may I make a point here? · As far as I see it, we have got two options. · I'd just like to say/point out that we can't afford the time. · In my opinion, it can't work at all. · Could I just say something? I (really) feel that … · In my opinion, it will be fine. · It's quite clear that we'll have to do it. · If you ask me … I tend to think that …
Soliciting opinions	· What do you think of the customer's claim? · How do you think we should deal with the issue? · What are your views on this?
Motion & vote	· I move that the proposal be withdrawn. · Let's put it to the vote. · I second the motion. · I'm for/against it. · I abstain(弃权)/object.

Agreeing/Disagreeing	· I agree/disagree with you on this point. · I'm afraid I don't see it like that. · I (can't) go along with you on that. Good point! I never thought about it that way before. · I get your point. · I see what you mean. · Up to a point I agree with you, but … · I'm afraid I can't agree with you. I think … · I must admit I never thought about … that way before. I have to agree with …
Closing a meeting	· Well, that seems to be all the time we have today. · Unfortunately, we're running short of time. We'll have to leave that to another time. · Thank you very much … Right, it looks as though we've covered the main items. Is there any other business? · I think we'd better leave that for another meeting. · The meeting is finished, we'll see each other next … · The meeting is closed. · I declare the meeting closed.

■ Task 2   Cultural salon

Read the following passage and try to get some knowledge about business meetings.

People seek conformity and harmony in collective cultures, where no one wants to make a showy display of his ability by taking up the initiative and priority. Mexico is a country thinking highly of collectivism. The behavior of the Mexicans' keeping silence and listening attentively shows their unwillingness to be the leading bird, for they know "the outstanding usually bear the brunt of attack". It is quite the other way round in Allan's culture, so he is surprised.

The Mexicans may become anxious about uncertainty and vagueness. They speak out their minds only when they are quite sure of the truth and the accuracy of an answer, for fear that they be scolded for the infeasibility of their ideas. So they prefer keeping silent to avoid mistakes. But to Allan, any constructive suggestions should be encouraged to elicit good ideas through brainstorming.

The Mexicans keep silent to show their deference to their supervisor. Otherwise, they will offend the authority by making suggestions. While in Allan's culture, all people are equal in work. There is no such division as the superior and the inferior, and what really matters is communication in work on a real equal basis.

This case tells us that in a cross-cultural working environment it is of necessity to know the cultural differences and take corresponding measures to make up the gaps. Only in this way, can the individual put his ability and talent into full play and can management not be frustrated due to cultural conflicts and gaps.

Unit Ten

International Exhibition

 Unit objectives

After learning this unit, you should
- find ways to improve your oral skills and performance;
- master basic words and expressions about international exhibitions;
- know some cultural background knowledge about international exhibitions.

Unit Ten International Exhibition

Preparing

I. Useful words and expressions

1. 博览会
2. 参展商情况
3. 参展程序
4. 展台工作人员
5. 多层展台
6. 参展商手册
7. 展出领域
8. 商展
9. 展区
10. 报名费
11. launch a new event
12. professional visitor
13. opening hour
14. sponsor
15. stand
16. theme zone
17. shuttle service
18. exhibition hall
19. free admission with an invitation
20. application procedure for holding an exhibition

II. Useful sentences

1. How do you think of the quality of our products?
2. We are always improving our design and patterns to confirm to the world market.
3. My offer was based on reasonable profit, not on wild speculations.
4. Would you accept delivery spread over a period of time?
5. In general, our prices are given on an FOB basis.

Situational conversations

Application & booth reservation

A: Good morning. Zara Exhibition Center. Can I help you?

B: Yes, please. I'm with Dola in the US. I'd like to register for the International Motorcycle Exhibition.

A: May I have your name, sir?

B: I'm Thomas Brown.
A: Let me check, Mr. Brown ... Thank you for waiting. Fortunately, there are still some booths available. If you send us your registration form and registration fees within two weeks, it is still possible for you to get one booth.
B: May I register for it now on the phone?
A: Sure. Which credit card would you like to use?
B: American Express.

Exhibition preparation

A: How is the preparation for the fair?
B: I am worried about the hall decoration.
A: Yes?
B: It should be completed by the next Monday and we have only one more week.
A: I think we will have to try our best. What about the transport of the exhibits?
B: So far so good! I think they'll be here on time.
A: Good. I want everything in good order before the fair. By the way, Miss Wang, the opening ceremony will be held on next Tuesday. Have all the visitors been notified?
B: Yes. I sent them formal invitations a week ago.
A: Have you prepared the guidebook, which includes the introduction and schedules of the fair?
B: Yes, I have. I have also prepared a fair memo.
A: Good. By the way, will you help me to type these letters and mail them immediately?
B: Yes, of course.

Exhibition reception

A: Good afternoon. I am Mr. Brown, the Import Manager of Atlantic Industries Ltd., Sydney, Australia. This is my card.
B: Good afternoon, Mr. Brown. My name is Mrs. Anderson, manager of the sales department.

A: Nice to see you, Mrs. Anderson.
B: Nice to see you too, Mr. Brown. Won't you sit down?
A: Thank you.
B: What would you like, tea or coffee?
A: I'd prefer coffee if you don't mind.
B: Is it your first trip to the Fair, Mr. Brown?
A: No, it's the fourth time.
B: Good. Are there any changes you find about the Fair?
A: Yes, a great deal. The business scope has been broadened, and there are more visitors than ever before.
B: Really, Mr. Brown? Did you find anything interesting?
A: Oh, yes. Quite a bit. But we are especially interested in your products.
B: We are glad to hear that. What items are you particularly interested in?
A: Women's dresses. They are fashionable and suit Australian women well, too. If they are of high quality and the prices are reasonable, we'll purchase large quantities of them. Will you please quote us a price?
B: All right.

Exhibition introduction

A: Good morning. My name is Mr. Brown. I'm from Australia. Here is my card.
B: Thank you. I'm pleased to meet you, Mr. Brown. My name is Lily, the representative of Green Textile Import and Export Corporation.
A: Pleased to meet you too, Lily. I travel a lot every year on business, but this is my first visit to your country. I must say I have been much impressed by your friendly people.
B: Thank you for saying so. Have you seen the exhibition halls? On display are most of our products, such as silk, woolen knitwear, cotton piece goods, and garments.
A: Oh, yes. I had a look yesterday. I found some of the exhibits to be fine in quality and beautiful in design. The exhibition has successfully displayed to me what your corporation handles. I've gone over the catalogue and the pamphlets

enclosed in your last letter, and I've had some knowledge about your export products. I'm quite interested in your silk blouses.

B: Our silk is known for its good quality. It is one of our traditional exports. Silk blouses are brightly colored and beautifully designed. They've met with great favor overseas and are always in great demand.

Exhibition negotiating

A: I'm glad to have the opportunity of visiting your corporation. I hope to conclude some substantial business with you.

B: It's a great pleasure to meet you, Mr. Wang. I believe you have seen our exhibits in the showroom. May I know what particular items you're interested in?

A: I'm interested in your hardware. I've seen the exhibits and studied your catalogues. I think some of the items will find a ready market in Canada. Here is a list of my requirements, for which I'd like to have your lowest quotations, CIF, Vancouver.

B: Thank you for your inquiry. Would you tell us the quantity you require so that we can work out the offers?

A: I'll do that. Meanwhile, could you give me an indication of price?

B: Here are our FOB price lists. All the prices in the lists are subject to our confirmation.

A: What about the commission? From European suppliers I usually get a three to five percent commission for my imports. It's the general practice.

B: As a rule, we don't allow any commission. But if the order is a substantial one, we'll consider it.

A: You see, but I do business on a commission basis. A commission on your prices would make it easier for me to promote sales. Even two or three percent would help.

B: That's something we can discuss later.

Exhibition effect

A: Mr. Li, what are the results of the exhibition?
B: Not bad.
A: Could you give me some details?
B: Yes. We have established business relationships with two new clients, who ordered 20 million RMB of cotton cheongsams.
A: Good. Are there any other achievements?
B: I also got acquainted with more than 200 customers.
A: Oh, wow. What is the effect?
B: Customers made more than ten suggestions. We held a product showing meeting and a press conference there. As a result, our brand has been strengthened.
A: Very good!
B: Here is the results analysis. I hope the visitors at the exhibition can be our real buyers in the future.
A: You are right. I think you've done an excellent job.

Oral practice

I. Talk with each other about the following questions or topics

1. What is the significance of exhibition for companies?

2. How can an organizer attract exhibitors and visitors to participate in the exhibition?

3. For the exhibitors, what should be included in the reports on the results of exhibition?

4. What should the exhibitors do to secure more orders after participating in an international exhibition?

II. Situational practice

1. Suppose you are the marketing manager of ABC Toys Co. Ltd. Your company is going to participate in Hong Kong Toys & Games Fair, which will be

held on 9 - 12 January, 2018 at Hong Kong Convention and Exhibition Centre. You are calling the organizer for detailed information of the fair and expressing your willingness to book an exhibition venue.

2. Suppose you are the marketing manager of Dechang Toys Co. Ltd., an exhibitor in the 16th Asia International Toys and Games Fair. The purchasing manager of Sydney Kids' Paradise, Stella Blair, is interested in your products. You are going to introduce your company and products to her. You should try your best to secure an order from her.

3. Suppose you are a sales representative of a Chinese electronic product company at the North Spring Trade Show. A Philippine dealer of electronic products, Winy Crews, is enquiring prices of your products.

Complementary reading

Text A

A: I'd like to get the ball rolling by talking about the price.

B: I'd be happy to answer any questions you may have.

A: Your products have very good quality. But I am a little worried about the prices you are asking.

B: You think we will be asking for more?

A: That's not exactly what I had in mind. I'd like 25% discount.

B: That seems to be a little high. I don't know how we can make profits with those numbers.

A: Well, if we promise future business—volume sales, that will lower the costs for making products, right?

B: Yes, but it's hard to see how you can order such large orders. We'd like a guarantee of future business, not just a promise.

A: We said we wanted 2,000 pieces over 6 months period with guarantee.

B: If you can guarantee that on paper, I think we can discuss this further.

Unit Ten International Exhibition

Text B

A: Hello, Martin.

B: Hello, Mr. Chen. Nice to see you again.

A: Sit down, please.

B: Thank you. I appreciate that you can share your time to meet me.

A: You're welcome.

B: My company needs more feedback from the consumers in order to improve our goods. Would you mind telling us about this?

A: Sure. We received the packs from you on the 15th of last month and it was intact. Very good.

B: Have you already used them?

A: Yes, we consider that the quality is quite good. However, in the manual book there are no indications with pictures. If there were, it would be easier for users to follow the directions.

B: I will propose it to the company. We may do it later. Thank you for your suggestion.

A: We are very satisfied with the good after-sales service.

B: Thank you for your support. Please take care of the business card and service card. If you have any problems or suggestions, please contact with us.

A: Your working attitude is very good.

B: Thanks for your praise. This is a card with the signature of our sales staff. We wish your company a prosperous future.

A: I appreciate that. Thank you for your visit.

B: Thank you for your valuable time. Goodbye!

Tasks

Task 1 Vocabulary development

Read the following words and expressions. Try to keep them in mind and find

more to enrich your language bank.

A. Useful words and expressions

长期,持续不断地	on a regular basis
底价	floor offer
讲清楚,清楚地说明	spell out
符合,依照	in line with
独家经销代理	exclusive selling agency
季节性折扣	seasonal discount
分期付款	payment by installment
随行就市	subject to market fluctuation
与你的竞争对手合作	cooperate with your competitor
例外一次	make an exception
艰难的商业谈判	difficult sales negotiation
半信半疑地	with a grain of salt
开始认真考虑	get down to
底线	bottom line
相对供应不足	in relatively short supply
输得一干二净	lose your shirt
达成协议	come to terms
提到,涉及	when it comes to
大计划,总方针	grand design
避免含混不清之处	avoid grey area
欺诈,玩弄	play loose with
活动开始	event set-up
吸引很多签约参加活动	draw adequate event sign-up
从事经营	conduct business
共同出资租用场地	chip in on venue rental
获得利益	gain mileage
增加活动的信誉度	boost the creditability of the event
确保授权进入	ensure authorized access
确认满意度	determine the satisfaction level

Unit Ten International Exhibition

大宗买进	buy in
(业务)级排行榜	tally of standings
销售完	close a sale
对等交换	peer-to-peer exchange
企业与企业之间的商务模式	business-to-business
不遗余力	spare no effort
多了解一些	know more about ...
进一步的信息	further information
官方媒体合作伙伴	official media partner
记者招待会,新闻发布会	press conference
主旨演说	keynote speech
有成本效益的,划算的	cost-effective

B. Sample sentences

Introduction	• What would be a nice location for our household electric appliances? • It provides very easy, convenient access for show attendees, exhibitors and freight delivery. • It caters to a variety of needs and interests. • We provide our clients with a whole package of services. • Choosing a suitable venue is the common wish of the organizers, undertakers and participants. • Choosing a venue that works best for your show involves many important considerations. • There are about 15,000 products on display. • The exhibit mainly consists of new products which have been produced by various factories. • The exhibition provides a unique opportunity for all exhibitors to meet, network, negotiate and conduct business.
Booth & register	• What would be a nice location for our exhibition? • When can we come to decorate our booth? • The average price of a standard booth is ... • We had better start out with some place close to our target clients. • Please reserve a booth for us. We will contact you as soon as possible.

	· We would like to register for the trade fair. · The estimated number of the booths is … · Are there any booths available? · The deadline for the registration is … · What are the least expensive booths you have?
Exhibition marketing	· What time would suit you best? · We must have respect for the needs of exhibitors. · We can assure you of our close cooperation. · Could I meet you in your company? · I think we may be able to work together in the future.
Promotion	· The company adheres to its policy of flexible and varied business operations. · Good quality and low price will help push the sales of our products. · We maintain a good relationship with clients through sincere communication and professional technique support. · I would like to say something about our company's market strategies and development strategies for the next few years. · Let me show you the new products for next year. Our price is the best. · This price is not our regular price. It's a special promotion. · We have a variety of products for you to select. · This type of machine is top of the line. · We will provide you with technical support if you have questions. · We can provide you with the service of installation free of charge. · If you are not satisfied, there will be no charge. · Shall we talk over the details after the show? · We will send free samples to our potential customers.
After exhibition	· Thank you for your consideration. I will think about your proposal and contact you. · You have done a lot for this exhibition. I hope we will have more chances to cooperate with each other. · It will be our great honor if it becomes a good memory for you. · I would like to reserve this location for next year. · During next year's show, I would like to have this spot again. · Next year, I would like a booth in the center. · Thank you for trying so hard. You are very thoughtful.

■ Task 2 Cultural salon

Read the following passage and try to get some knowledge about exhibitions.

About the exhibition

Best event planning guide

You should always go through the following procedures: First, you should analyze the event you are going to hold. Then, most important of all, the budget, you could only play and arrange all the event activities within the budget. Before operation, make sure that you always find some professionals and focus the event promotion. Don't forget the safety plans for the event and the afterwards clean-up.

Exhibition invitation

Exhibition invitation is the key step of exhibition marketing and a guarantee of a successful exhibition. Before the exhibition, various forms such as newspapers, telephones, faxes, e-mails, websites, mails, invitations, visits, etc. are used to invite related organizations of various places to be exhibitors or sponsors.

If you want to reach effective invitation, you should follow the processes below: you should determine the target clients from the databases and send invitations (e-mail, mail delivery, fax, etc.) and analyze delivery results. And don't forget the confirmation, telemarketing (telephone calls, reminders before the exhibition date). Furthermore, if there are some personal VIP invitations (market categorization by CRM methods), always make the confirmation properly.

Winning the client

The ultimate goal of an exhibition show is to sell the products. The process of receiving clients is also the process of selling. The last decision to buy is always caused by the first impression of the service. So to a businessman, some arts need to be learnt on how to receive clients or how to help the clients be glad to accept your products. When discussing receiving clients, we should get to know: winning clients themselves first, then deals and paying attention to body language and we should always be client-oriented. And a professional reception team is prerequisite.

Creating a powerful sales presentation

Make the presentation relevant to your prospect. And it could create a connection between your product/service and the prospect. Focus on the point. And you should always be animated. Showmanship should be applied also. And while presenting, don't forget the physical demonstration and lastly, have faith in your product/service all along.

Unit Eleven

Public Relations

 Unit objectives

After learning this unit, you should
- find ways to improve your oral skills and performance;
- master the basic words and expressions about public relations;
- know some cultural background knowledge about public relations.

Preparing

Ⅰ. Useful words and expressions

1. 雇员
2. 客户
3. 合作伙伴
4. 社区参与
5. 媒体
6. 售后服务
7. 分发传单
8. 公司处所
9. 赞助
10. 国际声誉
11. remuneration
12. remuneration package
13. promotion campaign
14. public speaking
15. launching of new products
16. merger with another company
17. embargo
18. press release
19. dignitary
20. publicity and press agentry

Ⅱ. Useful sentences

1. My job is to organize events on the monthly basis.
2. I am responsible for developing the company's reputation.
3. My job involves communication with the press.
4. In this job I have to establish relationships with the customers/clients.
5. I also have to prepare and supervise the company's external communication.
6. I'm responsible for creating brand awareness for the company's products.

Situational conversations

First visiting

A: Excuse me, is this the office of the Textile Corporation?
B: Yes, what can I do for you?
A: I'm from CBC Trade Company. Here is my card.
B: Welcome to our corporation. I'm in charge of the pubic relations.
A: I'm very glad to meet you here. You are Mr. ...

B: I'm Yang Kun. Please be seated.
A: Thank you, Mr. Yang. I'm here to discuss the possibility of establishing business relations with your corporation.
B: We'd be very glad to do so. Have you seen the exhibits displayed in the hall?
A: Yes, I found some of the exhibits to be excellent. I'm interested in those brightly colored and beautiful designed silks.
B: Silks are one of China's traditional exports and they are usually well received abroad.
A: Can you give me a price list with specifications?
B: Yes, of course. If you make an inquiry, we can make you a firm offer.

Postponing a meeting

A: Hello, is that Tom?
B: Yeah, it is me. So what's up, Linda?
A: Well, I am calling to reschedule our appointment on Sunday. I am afraid I can't make it that day.
B: Why? Is there anything wrong?
A: Yes. Yesterday my mom dropped off from the staircase and had her ribs broken.
B: Oh, I am quite sorry to hear that. Is she OK now?
A: She was taken to hospital immediately and is now under close watch.
B: So don't worry now. She is going to be fine.
A: Thanks, but what I am worrying now is that I will have to disappoint you this Sunday because I can't show up that day.
B: You mean you will have to stay with your mom that day?
A: I am afraid so. My father and sister are far away in America and I am consequently the only one to take care of her.
B: Yes, I can identify with you. If I were you, I would do the same.
A: Thank you so much for your understanding, Bob! What about postponing the meeting to next Thursday when our boss will be back from his meeting in Europe and will share with us some of his ideas about this business trip.

B: You mean we can take this chance to uncover to him our new plan?

A: Exactly!

B: That sounds great! So let's meet next Thursday! Oh, by the way, please bring my best regards to your mom.

A: Thanks, I will!

B: See you!

Complaints and solving problems

A: I have to dial up BC Trade now.

B: What's wrong?

A: Yesterday they called me and said that our latest shipment was delayed.

B: OK. You should call them, and see if you can get to the bottom of it.

A: Hello, may I speak to Amy Brown, please?

C: This is Amy. Hello, Bob?

A: I'm calling to ask what has happened. We received a message from your company that informed us of our delay. But after I checked out, we didn't.

C: Yes, we had contract in handing over the shipment today, right?

A: Yes, and we sent it out 7 days ago.

C: But we haven't received it yet.

A: You're saying our company is under a cloud for our credit?

C: I didn't say so, and I never mean that, Bob. I just mean we both should deliver on our appointment, and if there is something breaking out, we should dispose of it together.

A: OK. I bow to your explanation, but I have to claim it again that we sent our shipment on time. You may go and check it for another time.

Oral practice

I. Talk with each other about the following questions or topics

1. What are public relations?
2. What are public relations composed of?

3. What are the goals of positive public relations?
4. What is a press release?
5. How is a press release used?

II. Situational practice

1. Work in pairs. One acts as the manager of a Chinese company, and the other acts as a visitor from a famous company in Chicago. Two of you are exchanging some experience of dealing with the public relations of your own company. Make a dialogue.

2. Work in groups. Log on the Internet to find the public relations policy of one of the famous companies you are familiar with. Then make a public speech.

3. Miss Li, Mr. Gray's secretary, is talking to a visitor without an appointment. Mr. Gray is ready to go out for a meeting and doesn't have time to receive him. Make a dialogue.

4. Miss Lin, a secretary concerning foreign affairs, is asked to take care of the foreign guests invited to a banquet. Make a dialogue.

Complementary reading

Text A

Public relations professionals present the face of an organization or individual, usually to articulate its objectives and official views on issues of relevance, primarily to the media. Public relations contribute to the way an organization is perceived by influencing the media and maintaining relationships with stakeholders. According to Dr. Jacquie L'Etang from Queen Margaret University, public relations professionals can be viewed as "discourse workers specializing in communication and the presentation of argument and employing rhetorical strategies to achieve managerial aims".

Specific public relations disciplines include:
- Financial public relations—communicating financial results and business strategies.
- Consumer/Lifestyle public relations—gaining publicity for a particular product

or service.
- Crisis communication—responding in a crisis.
- Internal communication—communicating within the company itself.
- Government relations—engaging government departments to influence public policy.
- Media relations—a public relations function that involves building and maintaining close relationships with the news media so that they can sell and promote a business.
- Celebrity public relations—promotion of a celebrity to various media publications and outlets.
- Food-centric relations—communicating specific information centered on food, beverages and wine.

Text B

Reputation management refers to the influencing and controlling of an individual's or group's reputation. The growth of the Internet and social media, along with reputation management companies, have made search results a core part of an individual's or group's reputation.

Online reputation management, sometimes abbreviated as ORM, focuses on the management of product and service search results within the digital space. A variety of electronic markets and online communities like e-Bay, Amazon and Alibaba have ORM systems built in, using effective control nodes which can minimize the threat and protect systems from possible misuses and abuses by malicious nodes in decentralized overlay networks.

Tasks

Task 1 Vocabulary development

Read the following words and expressions. Try to keep them in mind and find more to enrich your language bank.

A. Useful words and expressions

crisis management	危机管理
be faced with complaints or problems	面对/面临投诉或问题
diffuse a negative situation quickly and effectively	迅速、有效地化解负面形势
come into contact with	与……联系
crisis communication	危机沟通
deal with major incidents	处理大事件
faulty product recall	（不良）缺陷产品召回
maintain its reputation	维持声誉
in the event of negative publicity	万一有负面报道
handle a situation	处理情况
make a negative comment	做出一个负面评论
on the whole	总的说来
generate publicity	产生公众效应
a positive promotional tool	积极的促销方式
take steps	采取措施
manage a crisis	管理危机,应对危机
spill over	蔓延,扩散
be likely to do	很可能做……
seek a negative comment	找到一个负面评论
refuse to comment	拒绝评论
be willing to do	愿意做……
a calculated lie	策划好的谎言
create a rumor	制造谣言
come to a conclusion	得出一个结论
put forward a fact	提供一个事实
show concern about the apparent victim	对直接受害人表示关切
avoid accepting responsibility	回避承担责任
mounting pressure	不断增加的压力
desire to make amends	提供补偿的愿望

be completely at odds with 与……完全矛盾
maintain a good two-way relationship 保持良好的双向关系

B. Sample sentences

Problem	• There's a problem with the circuitry on some of the units. • This will damage your reputation in the market place. • Your company failed to meet the terms of our agreement.
Apology	• It is entirely our fault. • I am very sorry about this confusion. • Please accept our sincere apology.
Promise	• I will get this sorted out immediately. • I will look into the case and report the result to you. • I shall send ... to the suppliers immediately. • We can guarantee that it won't happen again.

■ Task 2 Cultural salon

Read the following passage and try to get some knowledge about public relations.

Public relations

Public relations, commonly called PR, is the practice of managing the spread of information between an individual or an organization (such as a business, a government agency, or a nonprofit organization) and the public. It is also applied to the profession responsible for handling such assignments. The public vary from employees and stockholders to an entire community or members of the news media. The communication between an organization and its public ranges from a simple news release to a sophisticated campaign featuring films, advertisements, speeches, and television appearances. Such communication is aimed at gaining the goodwill of the public.

Public relations specialists establish and maintain relationships with an organization's target audience, the media, and other opinion leaders. Common responsibilities include designing communication campaigns, writing news releases and other content for news, working with the press, arranging interviews for company spokespeople, writing speeches for company leaders, acting as an organization's spokesperson, preparing clients for press conferences, media interviews and speeches, writing website and social media content, managing company reputation (crisis management), managing internal communication, and marketing activities like brand awareness and event management. Success in the field of public relations requires a deep understanding of the interests and concerns of each of the company's many stakeholders. The public relations professional must know how to effectively address those concerns using the most powerful tool of the public relations trade, which is publicity.

Unit Twelve

Transportation & Logistics

Unit objectives

After learning this unit, you should
- find ways to improve your oral skills and performance;
- master the basic words and expressions about transportation and logistics;
- know some cultural background knowledge about transportation and logistics.

Unit Twelve Transportation & Logistics

Preparing

Ⅰ. **Useful words and expressions**

1. 物流战略
2. 物流系统
3. 货物运输
4. 经营效率
5. 虚拟物流
6. 电子数据交换
7. 采购,购买
8. 物流成本
9. 物流网络
10. 联合运输
11. door to door
12. transfer transport
13. container transport
14. full container load (FCL)
15. tangible loss
16. bar code
17. less than container load (LCL)
18. logistics alliance
19. customized logistics
20. loading and unloading

Ⅱ. **Useful sentences**

1. I believe you're going out of your way to do it.

2. It is necessary to insure the goods against the possible risks they are exposed to in the course of transportation.

3. Because the goods are fragile, they should be wrapped in soft materials and firmly packed in cardboard boxes so as to reduce damage.

4. I wonder if it is possible to arrange shipping for us.

5. It usually takes us three months to make delivery. Everything will be ready by the middle of June.

Situational conversations

Introduction

A: Welcome to our company, sir. Nice to meet you.
B: Nice to meet you, too.
A: My name is Alex. It's very kind of you to visit our company. I'm very happy

to introduce it.

B: Thanks a lot.

A: Our business covers packaging, warehousing and shipping.

B: Do you ship door to door?

A: Certainly. All shipments are door to door!

B: Oh, I'm happy to hear that!

A: If you have any other questions, please feel free to contact me anytime.

B: Thanks a lot.

A: It's my pleasure.

Discussion about shipment

A: Hello, this is Pearl Logistics Company. I'm John Smith. What can I do for you?

B: I am willing to transport ten cartons of dresses from Qingdao to Boston. I want to discuss the shipment with you.

A: As to shipping, what's your idea?

B: We hope our customer can receive the goods as soon as possible. Generally speaking, it's faster to ship goods by train than by truck though it is more expensive.

A: If you require a carrier other than a truck, you must accept the additional charge.

B: I want to ask whether you can manage the goods in May.

A: Don't worry. We have no trouble in meeting your delivery date.

B: Since you promise that you will deliver the goods on time, we won't insist on the changing.

A: All right.

Discussion about more details

A: I am glad that we have an agreement with your company. At present, I want to know what your earliest delivery date is.

B: It usually takes us one month to deliver, and for a special order, it takes a little

Unit Twelve Transportation & Logistics

longer. It's about two months. In addition, prompt shipment is very important for us.

A: Our company has a lot of goods needing delivery. I think your company can do it best.

B: Oh ... Which kind of transportation do you want?

A: Uh ... Because we hope that our partner wouldn't miss the sales season, the sea transportation is the best.

B: Which shipping date is better for you?

A: I want to know the earliest time and we need to make sure the time.

B: We will try our best to advance shipment, but we cannot commit ourselves.

A: I'm glad to hear that. Thank you.

B: With kindest regard.

Feedback

A: This is Dora White. May I speak to your manager?

B: Hello, Ms. White. This is manager of QL (Quick Logistics). What can I do for you?

A: Oh, I have received my goods, but some boxes of the goods were damaged.

B: I'm sorry to hear that. If you have any questions about us, we will do our best to help you.

A: Thank you. On examination, 15 cases were found to be badly damaged.

B: We regret being unable to pay for that because the cases were in perfect condition when the goods were loaded.

A: According to the report, the damage was caused by your workers' rude moving.

B: This is important for us to keep reputation. Our workers are familiar with the progress about customers' goods. I hope your survey is unavailable.

A: Please calm down. We hope all disputes can be settled by communication.

B: Oh ... I hope so. I think we can make an agreement.

A: Yes, I think so. Thank you.

Oral practice

I. Talk with each other about the following questions or topics

1. What is the mission of logistics management?
2. How can a company gain competitive advantage through logistics?
3. What problems are there in the traditional logistics cost accounting system?

II. Situational practice

1. Suppose you are engaging in handling seasonal goods—air conditioners, and you wish to have your goods shipped earlier. Now you are going to urge your supplier to advance the shipment.

2. Mr. Wang wants to transport some tobacco as soon as possible and now he is having a talk with a carrier, discussing the details about road transportation.

Complementary reading

Text A

An increasing number of companies are involving in international markets through exporting, licensing, joint ventures, and ownership. This trend should continue. With such expansion there is a need to develop worldwide logistics networks. Integrated logistics management and cost analysis will be more complex and difficult to manage. There are some future trends in internationalization:

1. More logistics executives with international responsibilities.
2. Expansion of the number and size of foreign trade zones.
3. Reduction in the amount of international paperwork and documentation.
4. More foreign warehousing is owned and controlled by the exporting firm.
5. Increasing number of smaller firms.
6. Foreign ownership of logistics service firms, e.g., public warehousing and transportation carriers.
7. Increasing multiple distribution channels. The international transport and the

international logistics are the same thing in some way. So, when the international trading is involved, the firm must establish international logistics systems to provide the products and services demanded. The most significant development in international logistics will be the increasing sophistication information system adopted and the independent departments to operate.

Text B

The characters of modern logistics are huge quantity, quick response and globalization. In order to meet the needs, information technology has become the brain to control them. Bar code, POS, EDI, GPS and the Internet are the main choices for the operation of logistics. The bar code system can get the goods information fast and exactly. By the data processing unit, the POS system can check the inventory of warehouse at any time. When the super center adopts POS system, it can check the sales record, inventory even cash flow easily. EDI is a magic tool that can translate your documents into electronic data, and send it to your partner in any location by cable. In this way, we don't need to make a deal face to face. Revise the documents, declare to customs before the shipments arrived, and more. Now, EDI is the most essential information tool for international trade and logistics. All of the information tools are based on the Internet. In today's society, the organs of commercial and government, schools, even individuals can make E-commerce with the help of the Internet.

Tasks

Task 1 Vocabulary development

Read the following words and expressions. Try to keep them in mind and find more to enrich your language bank.

A. Useful words and expressions

    freight rate   运费率

    freight absorption   运费免收

volume of freight	货运量
dead freight	空舱费
freight agent	货运经理人
freight car	货车车厢
freight engine	货运机车
freight house	货栈，货仓
freight ton	运费吨
freight-in	进货运费
freight-out	销货运费
freight forward	运费由提货人支付
freight paid	运费付讫
freight prepaid	运费预付
by freight	用普通铁路货车运送
drag one's freight	离开，出发
additional freight	增列运费，附加运费
ad valorem freight	从价运费
advanced freight	预付运费
air freight	航空运费
logistics enterprise	物流企业
logistics document	物流单证
logistics alliance	物流联盟
supply logistics	供应物流
production logistics	生产物流
distribution logistics	销售物流
returned logistics	回收物流
waste material logistics	废弃物物流
environmental logistics	绿色物流

Unit Twelve Transportation & Logistics

B. Sample sentences

Inquiry about transportation	· How long does it take you to make delivery? · When will you dispatch the equipment we ordered to us? · Will it be possible for you to ship the goods on …? · What's the earliest time that you can effect your shipment?
Negotiation about transportation modes	· Is there any way to make an earlier shipment? · I wonder if you could ship the order as soon as possible. · What mode of transportation do you suggest we use? · What's your unloading port, please?
Specific requirement	· Please have the goods transported by sea. · I don't like this kind of combined transportation. · The bill of lading should be marked as "freight prepaid". · Who will bear the extra freight charges?
Complaint about transportation	· We have received none of the goods to this date. Please look into the matter and tell us the reason. · You know that time of delivery is very important to us. I hope you can give your special attention to our request.
Apology for being unable to meet the deadline	· I am afraid we can't make it/we can't promise delivery earlier than May 1st. · We won't be able to make shipment until next month. · I am sorry that we can't advance the time of delivery. · Sorry, we are unable to give you a definite date of shipment for the time being. · Given the tremendous pressure, please allow us one more week.

■ Task 2 Cultural salon

Read the following passage and try to get some knowledge about logistics.

Logistics

Logistics is generally a detailed organization and implementation of a complex operation. In a general business sense, logistics is the management of the flow of things between the point of origin and the point of consumption in order to meet requirements of customers or corporations. The resources managed in logistics can include physical items such as food, materials, animals, equipment, and liquids, as well as abstract items, such as time and information. The logistics of physical items usually involves the integration of information flow, material handling, production, packaging, inventory, transportation, warehousing, and often security.

In military science, logistics is concerned with maintaining army supply lines while disrupting those of the enemy, since an armed force without resources and transportation is defenseless. Military logistics was already practiced in the ancient world and as modern military have a significant need for logistics solutions, advanced implementation has been developed. In military logistics, logistics officers manage how and when to move resources to the places where they are needed.

Keys

Unit One

1. meet at the airport
2. I have heard a lot about you
3. have a nice journey
4. come all the way
5. recommend
6. hold a banquet in
7. bid farewell to
8. good memory
9. I feel honored to …
10. keep in touch
11. 纪念品
12. ……的象征
13. 欢迎词
14. 告别词
15. 热情好客
16. 周到的安排
17. 登记
18. 一切进展顺利
19. 领取行李
20. 适应时差

Unit Two

1. entertain
2. delicious cuisine
3. banquet
4. specialty
5. main course
6. appetizer
7. bottoms up
8. propose a toast
9. soft drink
10. dining etiquette
11. 你想要什么？
12. 味道很好
13. 吃得很饱
14. 代表
15. 为……健康着想
16. 请慢用
17. 自助宴会
18. 商业午餐
19. 丰盛的晚宴
20. 好客热情

Unit Three

1. airport terminal
2. duty-free shop
3. boarding pass（card）
4. single room
5. check in
6. identity card/ID card

7. suite
9. room service
11. 预订
13. 两张单人床
15. 结账离开
17. 淡季
19. 经济舱

8. reception clerk/receptionist
10. currency exchange service
12. 空房
14. 直达航班
16. 随身行李
18. 旺季
20. 信用卡

Unit Four

1. assistant
3. depth interview
5. married
7. birthplace
9. hobby
11. 个性
13. 主修课
15. 新闻时事
17. 职业规划
19. 学徒

2. probation
4. single
6. as requested
8. date of birth
10. work history
12. 简历
14. 应约
16. 两年的差距
18. 市场营销管理
20. 头条新闻

Unit Five

1. screen
3. be invited to a presentation
5. market research
7. accept an order
9. in a word
11. 商品特性
13. 订单
15. 没时间
17. 制造业
19. 运作

2. diagram
4. marketing approach
6. in the following sequence
8. quality control
10. share views
12. 顺序
14. 垄断
16. 利润
18. 服务业
20. 顾客满意度

Unit Six

1. brand

2. facility

3. account executive
4. acquisition
5. type of service
6. business administration
7. accrual
8. advertising
9. after-sales service
10. agent
11. 合并,重组
12. 分析家,化验员
13. 破产
14. 董事会
15. 中等品质
16. 财力
17. 财务报告
18. 固定成本
19. 手工业
20. 控股公司

Unit Seven

1. trial sale, test sale, test market
2. salable goods
3. selling line
4. sales agent
5. sales promotion
6. market segmentation
7. prospective customer
8. marketing mix
9. selling expense
10. seller's market
11. 现有顾客
12. 销售利润
13. 推销技术
14. 销售策略
15. 消费者促销活动
16. 销售预估
17. 货架陈列
18. 促销活动
19. 竞争品牌信息
20. 业绩目标

Unit Eight

1. irrevocable L/C
2. make a concession
3. remittance arrangement
4. deferred payment
5. accommodation
6. for your reference
7. remittance
8. D/P at sight
9. D/A
10. CIF/FOB
11. 唛头
12. 规定的条款
13. (资金)捆绑不流动
14. 现行的经济危机
15. 惯例
16. 以我方为受益人
17. 在中国议付
18. 汇票
19. 执行订单
20. 开具发票

Unit Nine

1. adjourn
2. agenda
3. in favor of
4. against
5. abstain
6. If you ask me, I tend to think that …
7. good point
8. I get your point
9. welcome meeting
10. 例会
11. 悬而未决
12. 达成共识/一致意见
13. 高层会谈
14. 通过友好会谈解决一切争端
15. 把某事提上日程
16. 会议记录
17. 会议记录员
18. 澄清某人立场

Unit Ten

1. expo
2. exhibitor's profile
3. participation procedure
4. booth personnel
5. multiple-story exhibit
6. exhibitor manual
7. scope of exhibit
8. trade show
9. exhibition area
10. registration fee
11. 举办一场新的活动
12. 业内人士
13. 开始时间
14. 主办者,赞助机构
15. 展位
16. 主题区
17. 接送服务
18. 展览馆
19. 凭请柬免费入场
20. 举办展览的申请程序

Unit Eleven

1. employee
2. customer/client
3. business partner
4. community involvement
5. media
6. after-sales service
7. distribute leaflets
8. company's premises
9. sponsorship
10. international reputation
11. 薪酬,报酬
12. 酬金措施
13. 推广活动,促销活动
14. 公共言论
15. 新产品的推出
16. 与其他公司合并
17. 贸易禁令
18. 新闻稿

19. 高官,显要人物

20. 信息传播和传媒工具

Unit Twelve

1. logistics strategy
2. logistics system
3. transport of goods
4. operational efficiency
5. virtual logistics
6. electronic data interchange (EDI)
7. procurement
8. logistics cost
9. logistics network
10. combined transport
11. 门到门
12. 中转运输
13. 集装箱运输
14. 整箱货
15. 有形消耗
16. 条码
17. 拼箱货
18. 物流联盟
19. 订制物流
20. 装卸